2—
9/24

DR. ACKERMAN'S BOOK OF THE YORKSHIRE TERRIER

LOWELL ACKERMAN DVM

BB-106

Overleaf: A pair of Yorkshire Terriers owned by Barbara Irwin. Photography by: Simi Ewing, Isabelle Francais, Judy Iby, Robert Pearcy, and Robert Smith.

The author has exerted every effort to ensure that medical information mentioned in this book is in accord with current recommendations and practice at the time of publication. However, in view of the ongoing advances in veterinary medicine, the reader is urged to consult with a veterinarian regarding individual health issues.

The presentation of pet products in this book is strictly for instructive purposes only; it does not necessarily constitute an endorsement by the author, publisher, owners of dogs portrayed, or any other contributors.

t.f.h.

©1996 by Lowell Ackerman DVM

Distributed in the UNITED STATES to the Pet Trade by T.F.H. Publications, Inc., One T.F.H. Plaza, Neptune City, NJ 07753; distributed in the UNITED STATES to the Bookstore and Library Trade by National Book Network, Inc. 4720 Boston Way, Lanham MD 20706; in CANADA to the Pet Trade by H & L Pet Supplies Inc., 27 Kingston Crescent, Kitchener, Ontario N2B 2T6; Rolf C. Hagen Inc., 3225 Sartelon St. Laurent-Montreal Quebec H4R 1E8; in CANADA to the Book Trade by Vanwell Publishing Ltd., 1 Northrup Crescent, St. Catharines, Ontario L2M 6P5 ; in ENGLAND by T.F.H. Publications, PO Box 15, Waterlooville PO7 6BQ; in AUSTRALIA AND THE SOUTH PACIFIC by T.F.H. (Australia), Pty. Ltd., Box 149, Brookvale 2100 N.S.W., Australia; in NEW ZEALAND by Brooklands Aquarium Ltd. 5 McGiven Drive, New Plymouth, RD1 New Zealand; in Japan by T.F.H. Publications, Japan— Jiro Tsuda, 10-12-3 Ohjidai, Sakura, Chiba 285, Japan; in SOUTH AFRICA by Lopis (Pty) Ltd., P.O. Box 39127, Booysens, 2016, Johannesburg, South Africa. Published by T.F.H. Publications, Inc.
MANUFACTURED IN THE
UNITED STATES OF AMERICA
BY T.F.H. PUBLICATIONS, INC.

BIOGRAPHY

D r. Lowell Ackerman is a world-renowned veterinary clinician, author, lecturer, and radio personality. He is a Diplomate of the American College of Veterinary Dermatology and is a consultant in the fields of dermatology, nutrition, and genetics. Dr. Ackerman is the author of 34 books and over 150 book chapters and articles. He also hosts a national radio show on pet health care and moderates a site on the World Wide Web dedicated to pet health care issues **(http://www.familyinternet.com/pet/pet-vet.htm)**.

BREED HISTORY

**THE GENESIS OF THE
MODERN YORKSHIRE TERRIER**

The Yorkshire Terrier has been bred since the mid-18th century but there is not much similarity between those dogs and the Yorkies of today. Britain was an agrarian society at that time and, with the  industrial revolution, Yorkshire began to develop as an industrial center with mills, factories, and coal mines.

Facing page: The Yorkshire Terrier is one of the best-loved breeds of both the American and British dog-fancying public.

It was a hard life for all who worked there and the dogs were no exception. We tend to think of the Yorkshire Terrier as a pampered housepet, but such was

Although we tend to think of Yorkshire Terriers as pampered housepets, they originally earned their keep catching rats and other small vermin. They remain hardy little dogs even today.

not always the case. Those early Terriers of Yorkshire earned their keep by catching rats and other small vermin.

The most distant known ancestor of the Yorkshire Terrier was probably either the Clydesdale Terrier, Waterside Terrier, or the Paisley Terrier. The Yorkshire Terrier eventually resulted from matings (selective or otherwise) with Toy Terriers, Skye Terriers, and Maltese Terriers. The Maltese Terriers were intentionally added to the mix to encourage long coats. There aren't any surviving records to confirm these crosses, likely because no breeding records were ever kept.

The first Yorkshire Terriers were registered in the British Kennel Club Stud Book in 1874 and the Club recognized Yorkies as an individual breed in 1886. About that same time, the Yorkshire Terrier was also becoming popular in the United States and Bradford Harry was the first Yorkie to become an American champion in 1889. Their popularity has continued to soar. Throughout the 1970s, the Yorkshire Terrier was the most popular dog in Britain. In 1994, the Yorkshire Terrier was the 11th most registered breed with the American Kennel Club.

Facing page: The Yorkshire Terrier resulted from matings of various breeds, including Maltese who were used to generate longer coats. Owner, Claudia Grunstra.

MIND & BODY

**PHYSICAL AND BEHAVIORAL TRAITS
OF THE YORKSHIRE TERRIER**

All Yorkshire Terriers know they're impor-tant: it's part of the Yorkie credo. The true Yorkie carries his head up, his tail high, and his heart on his sleeve. These are adoring,

charming companion dogs that will flourish and reward all who know them if treated with respect and intelligence.

Facing page: Of all the toy breeds, there is no finer pet than the Yorkshire Terrier. He is small, sturdy, and absolutely lovable. Owner, Nancy Kornick.

The Yorkshire Terrier is indeed a terrier, despite his toy size. He is vigorous and active, conducting himself in a confident way that befits his spirited, noble disposition.

CONFORMATION AND PHYSICAL CHARACTERISTICS

This is not a book about show dogs, so information here will not deal with the conformation of champions and how to select one. The purpose of this chapter is to provide basic information about the stature of a Yorkshire Terrier and qualities of a physical nature.

Clearly, beauty is in the eye of the beholder. And, since standards come and standards go, measuring your dog against some imaginary yardstick does little for you or your dog. Just because your dog isn't a show champion doesn't mean that he or she is any less of a family member. And, just because a dog is a champion doesn't mean that he or she is not a genetic time bomb waiting to go off.

When breeders and those interested in showing Yorkshire Terriers are selecting dogs, they are looking for those qualities that match the breed "standard." This standard, however, is of an imaginary Yorkshire Terrier and it changes from time to time and from country to coun-

Yorkshire Terriers are indeed terriers, despite their small size; they are vigorous and active.

try. Thus, the conformation and physical characteristics that pet owners should concentrate on are somewhat different and much more practical.

Yorkshire Terriers are small dogs and most show varieties will not exceed seven pounds. It is not unusual to see larger Yorkies as pets, however. They also have lovely tails unless there is surgical intervention. Be aware that it is not necessary to dock tails in the Yorkshire Terrier for it to be a purebred. Being a true Yorkshire Terrier has to do with genetics, not surgery. For those wanting to indulge, tails and dewclaws tend to be docked when pups are three to five days old. Most veterinary associations and even many breed registries are against altering animals to create an artificial image. Consider carefully your rationale if you decide to have these procedures done.

COAT COLOR, CARE, AND CONDITION

The "approved" color of the Yorkshire Terrier is steel blue with tan points. This is controlled by three primary gene pairs. Without becoming geneticists we can still appreciate how the color occurs in the breed with some basic rules. Each pup receives half a set of genes from its mother

Yorkshire Terriers are small dogs, and most show dogs do not exceed seven pounds. This four-week-old Yorkie puppy is tiny enough to fit into a shirt pocket. Owner, Wendy Garcia.

and half from its father. The Agouti series (A) determines the color of the hair pigment granules. Yorkies only have two possibilities here, both of which result in a saddle pattern ($a^{sa}a^{sa}$ or $a^{sa}a^{t}$). Next, to achieve the "blue" coloration, all Yorkies carry the double-recessive dilution gene pair (dd). Finally, the G series causes a gradual silvering of the coat as the dog matures and gets older. Here the Yorkie maintains the dominant pairing of GG.

Yorkshire Terriers are not for you if you would like a maintenance-free breed of dog. If you want them to maintain the coat

Keeping the Yorkshire Terrier's beautiful long coat looking its best requires daily attention. This dog has his coat wrapped in paper in order to prevent the ends of the hairs from breaking off, ensuring an undamaged long coat.

for which they are famous, daily attention is required. Show dogs are required to have long, straight, silky coats and this is not practical for anyone with a hectic lifestyle. If you find it relaxing and therapeutic to groom your animal daily, this is the breed for you. For those that enjoy the breed but don't enjoy the grooming aspects, there are a variety of "cuts" that make the coat more manageable. Even then, brushing must be done several days a week to control matting, and a bath every week is not excessive. Even with a short clip, trimming is required every four to six weeks.

The fur of the Yorkie is very much like human hair and requires the same amount of attention. Despite all of the work required, there are some benefits because this long-haired house pet isn't much of a shedder. Because of its lack of significant undercoat, shedding really isn't the problem most people anticipate.

BEHAVIOR AND PERSONALITY OF THE ACTIVE YORKSHIRE TERRIER

Behavior and personality are two qualities that are hard to standardize within a breed. Although generalizations are difficult to make, most Yorkshire Terriers are alert, friendly, intuitive, and people-oriented. This is not the breed to be kept in a kennel situation and deprived from regular contact with people.

Behavior and personality are incredibly important in dogs and there seem to be quite evident extremes in the Yorkshire Terrier. The earliest of the breed were bred for hunting down rats, but today's Yorkshire Terriers are more accustomed to being pampered pets that will go wherever their owners take them. Yorkshire Terriers are high-energy dogs but not typically high-strung. They like to play with people and other pets but they can be possessive and domineering, even with larger dogs. Today's Yorkshire Terriers seem far removed from their earliest

Yorkshire Terriers are high-energy dogs that love to play with people. These three Yorkies eagerly await treats from their owner.

Young children should be instructed to treat tiny Yorkshire Terriers gently and should always be supervised when they are with them. Dustin gingerly says hello to a new Yorkie friend.

your lap, most enjoy having a purpose in their day and that makes them excellent companions. They do not need long daily walks but they do appreciate events that involve family members. Show dogs usually have a different type of lifestyle because of their long tresses. Most breeders of these glamour dogs wouldn't let them play in a park or swim in the pool; the grooming consequences would be substantial. Fortunately, the pet Yorkshire Terrier doesn't have these constraints. All Yorkshire

ancestors. Because the Yorkshire Terrier is a high-energy dog and can cause much damage, it is worth spending the time when selecting a pup to pay attention to any evidence of personality problems. It is also imperative that all Yorkshire Terriers be obedience trained. Like any dog, they have the potential to be unruly without appropriate training; consider obedience classes mandatory for your sake and that of your dog.

Although many Yorkshire Terriers are happy to sleep the day away in bed, on the sofa, or on

Your Yorkshire Terrier will make a great walking partner; however, you must remember that his small little legs cannot go too fast or too far.

Many owners allow their pillow-sized Yorkies on to their beds. If you do not want your dog on your bed, you must enforce this rule starting at a young age.

Terriers should attend obedience classes and they need to learn limits to unacceptable behaviors. A well-loved and well-controlled Yorkshire Terrier is certain to be a valued family member.

For pet owners, there are several activities to which your Yorkshire Terrier is well-suited. They not only make great walking partners but they are also excel-lent community volunteers. Yorkshire Terriers are loyal and loving; aggressiveness and viciousness do not fit into the equation.

For Yorkshire Terrier enthusiasts who want to get into more competitive aspects of the dog world, showing and obedience are activities that can be considered.

SELECTING

**WHAT YOU NEED TO KNOW TO FIND
THE BEST YORKSHIRE TERRIER PUPPY**

Owning the perfect Yorkshire Terrier rarely happens by accident. On the other hand, owning a genetic dud is almost always the result of an impulsive purchase and  failure to do basic research. Buying this book is a major step in understanding the situation and making intelligent choices.

Facing Page:
Although Yorkshire Terrier puppies are absolutely adorable and irresistible, the decision to own one should be made with careful consideration and much research.

can't rely on any one source because there are no standards by which judgments can be made. Most veterinarians will recommend that you select a "good breeder" but there is no way to identify such an individual. A breeder of champion show dogs may also be a breeder of genetic defects.

The best approach is to select a pup from a source that regularly performs genetic screening and has documentation to prove it. If you are intending to be a pet owner, don't worry about whether your pup is show quality. A mark here or there that might disqualify the pup as a show winner has absolutely no impact on its ability to be a loving and healthy pet. Also, the vast majority of dogs will be neutered and not used for breeding anyway. Concentrate on the things that are important.

A good breeder cares about where she places her Yorkshire puppies. Be sure to do your homework before selecting the source of your new puppy. Owner, Carol Confer.

SOURCES

Recently, a large survey was done to determine whether there were more problems seen in animals adopted from pet stores, breeders, private owners, or animal shelters. Somewhat surprisingly, there didn't appear to be any major difference in total number of problems seen from these sources. What was different were the kinds of problems seen in each source. Thus, you

MEDICAL SCREENING

Whether you are dealing with a breeder, a breed rescue group, a shelter, or a pet store, your approach should be the same. You want to identify a Yorkshire Terrier that you can live with and screen it for medical and behavioral problems before you make it a permanent family member. If the source you select has not done the important testing needed, make sure they will offer you a health/temperament guarantee before you remove the dog from the premises to have the work done yourself. If this is not acceptable, or they are offering an exchange-only policy, keep moving; this isn't the right place for you to get a dog. As soon as you purchase a Yorkshire Terrier, pup or adult, go to your veterinarian for thorough evaluation and testing.

Pedigree analysis is best left to true enthusiasts but there are some things that you can do, even as a novice. Inbreeding is to be discouraged, so check out your four or five generation pedigree and look for names that appear repeatedly. Most breeders linebreed, which is acceptable, so you may see the same *prefix* many times but not the same actual dog or bitch. Reputable breeders will usually not allow inbreeding at least three generations back in the puppy's pedigree. Also ask the breeder to provide OFA and CERF registration numbers on all ancestors in the pedigree for which testing is done. If there

Yorkshire puppies are born black; black hairs are gradually replaced with tan as the dogs mature. This six-week-old bunch is beginning to develop the rich tan markings characteristic of the breed.

These two young Yorkies are ready to take on the world. Puppies should not be allowed outdoors until they are fully vaccinated and should never be outside unsupervised.

are a lot of gaps, the breeder has some explaining to do.

The screening procedure is easier if you select an older dog. Animals can be registered for hips and elbows as young as two years of age by the Orthopedic Foundation for Animals (OFA) and by one year of age by Genetic Disease Control (GDC). This is your insurance against hip dysplasia and elbow dysplasia later in life. Although Yorkshire Terriers now have a relatively low incidence of these orthopedic problems, it is because of the efforts of conscientious breeders who have been doing the appropriate testing. A verbal testimonial that they've never heard of the condition in their lines is not adequate and probably means they really don't know if they have a problem. Move along.

Evaluation is somewhat more complicated in the Yorkshire Terrier puppy. The PennHip™ procedure can determine risk for developing hip dysplasia in pups as young as 16 weeks of age. For pups younger than that, you should request copies of OFA or GDC registration for both parents. If the parents haven't both been registered, their hip and elbow status should be considered unknown and questionable.

All Yorkshire Terriers, regardless of age, should be screened for evidence of von Willebrand's disease. This can be accomplished with a simple blood test. The incidence is high enough in the breed that there is no excuse for not performing the test.

For animals older than one year of age, your veterinarian may also want to take a blood sample for a health status check. A heartworm test, urinalysis, and evaluation of feces for internal parasites should also be done. If there are any patches of hair loss, a skin scraping should be taken to determine if the dog has evidence of demodectic mange.

Your veterinarian should also perform a very thorough ophthalmologic (eye) examination. The most common eye problems in Yorkshire Terriers are cataracts, persistent pupillary membranes, and retinal dysplasia. It is best to acquire a pup whose parents have both been screened for heritable eye diseases and certified "clear" by organizations such as the Canine Eye Registration Foundation (CERF). If this has been the case, an examination by your veterinarian is probably sufficient and referral to an ophthalmologist is only necessary if recommended by your veterinarian.

BEHAVIORAL SCREENING

Medical screening is important, but don't forget temperament. More dogs are killed each year for behavioral reasons than for all medical problems combined. Temperament testing is a valuable although not infal- undesirable behaviors. Although not all behaviors are evident in young pups (e.g., aggression often takes many months to manifest itself), detecting anxious and fearful pups (and avoiding them) can be very important in the selection process.

Puppies should remain with their mother until nine to ten weeks of age. They should be allowed to nurse for at least six weeks before they are completely weaned from their mother. Owner, Simi Ewing.

lible tool in the screening process. The reason that temperament is so important is that many dogs are eventually destroyed because they exhibit undesirable behaviors. Traits most identifiable in the young pup include fear, excitability, low pain threshold, extreme submission, and noise sensitivity.

Pups can be evaluated for temperament as early as seven to eight weeks of age. Some behaviorists, breeders, and trainers recommend objective testing where scores are given in several different categories. Others are more casual about the process since it is only a crude indicator. In general, the evalua-

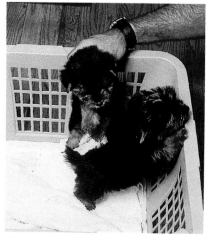

Breeders must socialize their Yorkie puppies and acclimate them to human contact once they are a few weeks old. Breeders will not permit potential buyers to touch the pups until the first set of inoculations. Owner, Marie Larkin.

tion takes place in three stages by someone the pup has not been exposed to. The testing is not done within 72 hours of vaccination or surgery. First, the pup is observed and handled to determine its sociability. Puppies with obvious undesirable traits such as shyness, hyperactivity, or uncontrollable biting may turn out to be unsuitable. Second, the desired pup is separated from the others and then observed for how it responds when played with and called. Third, the pup should be stimulated in various ways and its responses noted. Suitable activities include lying the pup on its side, grooming it, clipping its nails, gently grasping it around the muzzle, and testing its reactions to noise. In a study conducted at the Psychology Department of Colorado State University, it was also found that heart rate was a good indicator in this third stage of evaluation. Actually, they noted the resting heart rates, stimulated the pups with a loud noise and measured how long it took the heart rates to recover to resting levels. Most pups recovered within 36 seconds. Dogs that took considerably longer were more likely to be anxious.

Puppy Aptitude Tests (PAT) can be given in which a numerical score is given for 11 different traits, with a "1" representing the most assertive or aggressive expression of a trait and a "6" representing disinterest, independence, or inaction. The traits

Temperament tests are helpful indicators in determining the personality of the Yorkie pup you choose and can be done around eight weeks of age. This pup is obviously too pooped to be evaluated.

assessed in the PAT include social attraction to people, following, restraint, social dominance, elevation (lifting off ground by evaluator), retrieving, touch sensitivity, sound sensitivity, prey/chase drive, stability, and energy level. Although the tests do not absolutely predict behaviors, they do tend to do well at predicting puppies with behavioral extremes.

ORGANIZATIONS YOU SHOULD KNOW ABOUT

Project TEACH™ (Training and Education in Animal Care and Health) is a voluntary accreditation process for those individuals selling animals to the public. It is administered by Pet Health Initiative, Inc. (PHI) and provides instruction on genetic screening as well as many other aspects of proper pet care. TEACH-accredited sources screen animals for a variety of medical, behavioral, and infectious diseases before they are sold. Project TEACH™ supports the efforts of registries, such as OFA, GDC, and CERF, and recommends that all animals sold be registered with the appropriate agencies. For more information on Project TEACH™, send a self-addressed stamped envelope to Pet Health Initiative, P.O.

Box 12093, Scottsdale, AZ 85267-2093.

The Orthopedic Foundation for Animals (OFA) is a non-profit organization established in 1966 to collect and disseminate information concerning orthopedic diseases of animals and to establish control programs to lower the incidence of these diseases. A registry is maintained for both hip dysplasia and elbow dysplasia. The ultimate purpose of OFA certification is to provide information to dog owners to assist in the selection of good breeding animals; therefore, attempts to get a dysplastic dog certified will only hurt the breed by perpetuation of the disease. For more information contact your veterinarian or the Orthopedic Foundation for Animals, 2300 Nifong Blvd., Columbia, MO 65201.

The Institute for Genetic Disease Control in Animals (GDC) is a nonprofit organization founded in 1990 and maintains an open registry for orthopedic problems but does not compete with OFA. In an open registry like GDC, owners, breeders, veterinarians, and scientists can trace the genetic history of any particular dog once that dog and close relatives have been registered. At the present time, GDC operates open registries for hip dysplasia, elbow dysplasia, and osteochondrosis. GDC is currently developing guidelines for registries of Legg-Calve-Perthes disease, craniomandibular osteopathy, and medial patellar luxation. For more information, contact the Institute for Genetic Disease Control in Animals, P.O. Box 222, Davis, CA 95617.

The Canine Eye Registration Foundation (CERF) is an international organization devoted to eliminating hereditary eye diseases from purebred dogs. This organization is similar to OFA that helps eliminate diseases like hip dysplasia. CERF is a non-profit organization that screens and certifies purebreds as free of heritable eye diseases. Dogs are evaluated by veterinary eye specialists and findings are then submitted to CERF for documentation. The goal is to identify purebreds without heritable eye problems so they can be used for breeding. Dogs being considered for breeding programs should be screened and certified by CERF on an annual basis since not all problems are evident in puppies. For more information on CERF, write to CERF, SCC-A, Purdue University, West Lafayette, IN 47907.

The pick of the litter. A Yorkshire Terrier puppy should be alert and curious about its surroundings.

FEEDING & NUTRITION

**WHAT YOU MUST CONSIDER EVERY DAY TO FEED
YOUR YORKSHIRE TERRIER THROUGH HIS LIFETIME**

Nutrition is one of the most important aspects of raising a healthy Yorkshire Terrier and yet it is often the source of much controversy between breeders, veterinarians, pet owners, and dog food manufacturers. However, most of these arguments have more to do more with marketing than with science.

Facing page: This hungry Yorkshire pup pokes his head out of a lunch bag—obviously looking for something to eat. It is not a good idea, however, to feed your puppy human food.

Let's first take a look at dog foods and then determine the needs of our dog. This chapter will concentrate on feeding the pet Yorkshire Terrier rather than the breeding or working animals.

COMMERCIAL DOG FOODS

Most dog foods are sold based on marketing (i.e., how to make a product appealing to owners while meeting the needs of dogs). Some foods are marketed on the basis of their protein content, others based on a "special" ingredient, and some are sold because they don't contain certain ingredients (e.g., preservatives, soy). We want a dog food that specifically meets our dog's needs, is economical, and causes few, if any, problems. Most foods come in dry, semi-moist, and canned forms. Some can now be purchased frozen. The "dry" foods are the most economical, contain the least fat, and the most preservatives. The canned foods are the most expensive (they're 75% water), usually contain the most fat, and have the least preservatives. Semi-moist foods are expensive and high in sugar content, and I do not recommend them for any dogs.

When you're selecting a commercial diet, make sure the food has been assessed by feeding trials for a specific life stage, not just by nutrient analysis. This statement is usually located not far from the ingredient label. In the United States, these trials are performed in accordance with the American Association of Feed Control Officials (AAFCO) and, in Canada, by the Canadian Veterinary Medical Association. This certification is important because it has been found that dog foods currently on the market that provide only chemical analyses and calculated values, but no feeding trials, may not provide adequate nutrition. The feeding trials show that the diets meet minimal, not optimal, standards. However, they are the best tests we currently have.

PUPPY REQUIREMENTS

Soon after pups are born, and certainly within the first 24 hours, they should begin nursing from their mother. This provides them with colostrum, which is an antibody-rich milk that helps protect them from infection for their first few months of life. Pups should be allowed to nurse for at least six weeks before they are completely weaned from their mother. In the first three weeks of life, Yorkies are also prone to neonatal hypoglycemia (low blood sugar) because they have limited glycogen reserves and their liver enzymes are not fully functional. Most breeders are aware of this condition and monitor closely for it. Supplemental feeding may be started by as early as three weeks of age.

pups or provide them with "performance" rations. Overfeeding Yorkshire Terriers can lead to serious skeletal defects such as osteochondrosis, hip dysplasia, and perhaps Legg-Calve-Perthes disease.

Yorkshire Terriers are prone

Nursing pups receive colostrum from their mother. Colostrum is an antibody-rich milk that helps protect the pups from infection for their first few weeks of life.

By two months of age, pups should be fed puppy food. They are now in an important growth phase. Nutritional deficiencies and/or imbalances during this time of life are more devastating than at any other time. Also, this is not the time to overfeed

to hypoglycemia (low blood sugar) because they are small and have little in the way of reserves. This can result in trembling, nervousness, and seizures, and this condition must be addressed immediately. To differentiate transient hypoglycemia

For young puppies, mix dry kibble with water in order to make a soft mixture that is easier for them to eat.

from some congenital diseases, a blood glucose level is taken. Animals with transient hypoglycemia have low blood sugar levels and the symptoms disappear with treatment. Treatment includes making sure the animal has access to food if it will still eat or rubbing dextrose, corn syrup, or fruit juice into its gums. Do not attempt to force feed these products. Depending on response, your veterinarian will likely want to admit the pup to the hospital and start feeding by orogastric tube or intravenous therapy. Reducing stress is also important and a warm, quiet environment with constant nursing care is preferred.

Pups should be fed "growth" diets until they are 9–12 months of age. Pups will initially need to be fed 2–3 meals daily until they are 12 months old, then once to twice daily (preferably twice) when they are converted to adult food. Proper growth diets should be selected based on acceptable feeding trials designed for growing pups. If you can't tell by reading the label, ask your veterinarian for feeding advice.

Remember that pups need "balance" in their diets and avoid the temptation to supplement with protein, vitamins, or minerals. Calcium supplements have been implicated as a cause of bone and cartilage deformity, especially in large breed puppies. Puppy diets are already heavily fortified with calcium, and supplements tend to unbalance the mineral intake. There is more than adequate proof that these supplements are responsible for many bone deformities seen in growing dogs.

ADULT DIETS

The goal of feeding adult dogs is one of "maintenance." They have already done the growing they are going to do and are unlikely to have the digestive problems of elderly dogs. In general, dogs can do well on maintenance rations containing predominantly plant- or animal-based ingredients as long as that ration has been specifically formulated to meet maintenance level requirements. This contention should be supported by studies performed by the manufacturer in accordance with AAFCO (American Association of Feed Control Officials). In Canada, these products should be certified by the Canadian Veterinary Medical Association to meet maintenance requirements.

There's nothing wrong with feeding a cereal-based diet to dogs on maintenance rations and they are the most economical. When comparing maintenance rations, it must be appreciated that these diets must meet the "minimum" requirements for confined dogs, not necessarily optimal levels. Most dogs will benefit when fed diets containing easily-digested ingredients that provide nutrients at least slightly above minimum requirements. Typically, these foods will be intermediate in price between the most expensive super-premium diets and the cheapest generic diets. Select only those diets that have been substantiated by feeding trials to meet maintenance requirements, those that contain wholesome ingredients, and those recommended by your veterinarian. Don't select based on price, company advertising, or total protein content.

GERIATRIC DIETS

Yorkshire Terriers are considered elderly when they are about seven years of age and there are certain changes that occur as dogs age that alter their nutritional requirements. As pets age, their metabolism slows and this must be accounted for. If maintenance rations are fed in the same amounts while metabolism is slowing, weight gain may result. Obesity is the last thing one wants to contend with in an elderly pet, since it increases their risk of several other health-related problems. As pets age, most of their organs do not function as well they did in youth. The digestive system, the liver,

The goal of feeding your adult Yorkshire Terrier is one of maintenance. Most dogs benefit from foods that contain easily digested ingredients and provide nutrients at least slightly above minimum requirements.

the pancreas, and the gallbladder are not functioning at peak effect. The intestines have more difficulty extracting all the nutrients from the food consumed. A gradual decline in kidney function is considered a normal part of aging.

A responsible approach to geriatric nutrition is to realize that degenerative changes are a normal part of aging. Our goal is to minimize the potential damage by taking this into account while the dog is still well. If we wait until an elderly dog is ill before we change the diet, we have a much harder job.

Elderly dogs need to be treated as individuals. While some benefit from the nutrition found in "senior" diets, others might do better on the highly-digestible puppy and super-premium diets. These latter diets provide an excellent blend of digestibility and amino acid content but, unfortunately, many contain more salt and phosphorus than the older pet really needs.

Older dogs are also more prone to developing arthritis and therefore it is important not to overfeed them since obesity puts added stress on the joints. For animals with joint pain, supplementing the diet with fatty acid combinations containing cis-linoleic acid, gamma-linolenic acid, and eicosapentaenoic acid can be quite beneficial.

MEDICAL CONDITIONS AND DIET

Snacks are important for dogs because they represent a bonding experience with their owners (and because they enjoy them). However, snacks can be problematic for small dogs such as the Yorkshire Terrier. These small dogs are often considered "picky" eaters. Snacks can contribute to the problem of them not eating enough of their regular diets. Since a small dog may require about 500 calories (kcal) a day for maintenance and since many biscuit treats contain 60–100 calories apiece, it doesn't take too many treats to unbalance a feeding regimen. Thus, a small Yorkie eating only three biscuit treats a day should not be expected to eat a full meal; he's getting half his daily calories in treats! Therefore, give treats in moderation and consider low-calorie alternatives such as carrots.

Fat supplements are probably the most common supplements purchased from pet supply stores. They frequently promise to add luster, gloss, and sheen to the coat, and consequently make dogs look healthy. The only fatty acid that is essential for this purpose is cis-linoleic acid, which is found in flaxseed oil, sunflower seed oil, and safflower oil. Corn oil is a suitable but less effective alternative. Most of the other oils found in retail supplements are high in saturated and monoun-saturated fats and are not beneficial for shiny fur or healthy skin. For dogs with allergies, arthritis, high blood pressure (hypertension), high cholesterol, and some heart ailments, other fatty acids may be prescribed by a veterinarian.

The important ingredients in these products are gamma-linolenic acid (GLA), eicosapentaenoic acid (EPA), and docosa-hexaenoic acid (DHA). These products have gentle and natural anti-inflammatory properties. But don't be fooled by imitations. Most retail fatty acid supplements do not contain these functional forms of the essential fatty acids—look for gamma-linolenic acid, eicosa-pentaenoic acid, and docosah-exaenoic acid on the label.

Offer a Yorkie a yummy chicken-flavored Nylabone® to satisfy his chewing needs. These bones contain real chicken meal and are irresistible to dogs.

HEALTH

**PREVENTIVE MEDICINE AND HEALTH CARE
FOR YOUR YORKSHIRE TERRIER**

Keeping your Yorkshire Terrier healthy requires preventive health care. This is not only the most effective but the least expensive way to battle illness. Good preventive

care starts even before puppies are born. The dam should be well cared for, vaccinated, and free of infections and parasites.

Facing page: It is important for your Yorkshire Terrier's well-being to select a friendly reputable veterinarian that you can trust to provide good preventive health care.

Hopefully, both parents were screened for important genetic diseases (e.g., von Willebrands's disease), were registered with the appropriate agencies (e.g., OFA, GDC, CERF), showed no evidence of medical or behavioral problems, and were found to be good candidates for breeding. This gives the pup a good start in life. If all has been planned well, the dam will pass on to her pups a resistance to disease that will last for their first few months of life. However, the dam can also pass on parasites, infections, genetic diseases, and more.

TWO TO THREE WEEKS OF AGE

By two to three weeks of life, it is usually necessary to start pups on a regimen to control worms. Although dogs benefit from this parasite control, the primary reason for doing this is human health. After whelping, the dam often sheds large numbers of worms even if she has previously tested negative. This is because many worms lay dormant in tissues and the stress of delivery causes parasites to be released and shed into the environment. Assume that all puppies potentially have worms, because studies have shown that 75% do. Thus, we institute worm control early to protect the people in the house from worms, more than the pups themselves. The deworming is repeated every two to three weeks until your veterinarian feels the condition is under control. Nursing bitches

All puppies should have a chance to socialize with their littermates, and Yorkies are no exception. This will help them when they come in contact with other dogs later in life.

should be treated because they often shed worms during this time. Only use products recommended by your veterinarian. Over-the-counter parasiticides have been responsible for deaths in pups.

SIX TO TWENTY WEEKS OF AGE

Most puppies are weaned from their mother at six to eight weeks of age. Weaning shouldn't be done too early so that pups have the opportunity to socialize with their littermates and dam. This is important for them to be able to respond to other dogs later in life. There is no reason to rush the weaning process unless the dam can't produce enough milk to feed the pups.

Pups are usually first examined by the veterinarian at six to eight weeks of age, which is when most vaccination schedules commence. If pups are exposed to many other dogs at this young age, veterinarians often opt for vaccinating with inactivated parvovirus at six weeks of age. When exposure isn't a factor, most veterinarians would rather wait to see the pup at eight weeks of age. At this point, they can also do a preliminary dental evaluation to see that all the puppy teeth are coming in

correctly, check to see that the testicles are properly descending in males, and make sure that there are no health reasons to prohibit vaccination at this time. Heart murmurs, wandering knee-caps (luxating patellae), juvenile cataracts, and her-

Assume that all puppies potentially have worms and institute worm control early, around two to four weeks of age.

nias are usually evident by this time.

Your veterinarian may also be able to perform temperament testing on the pup by eight weeks of age, or recommend someone to do it for you. Although temperament testing is not completely accurate, it can often predict which pups are most anxious and fearful. Some form of temperament evaluation is important because behavioral problems account for more animals being euthanized (killed) each year than all medical conditions combined.

Recently, some veterinary hospitals have been recommending neutering pups as early as six to eight weeks of age. A study done at the University of Florida College of Veterinary Medicine over a span of more than four years concluded there was no increase in complications when animals were neutered when less than six months of age. The evaluators also concluded that the surgery appeared to be less stressful when done in young pups.

Most vaccination schedules consist of injections being given at 6–8, 10–12, and 14–16 weeks of age. Ideally, vaccines should not be given closer than two weeks apart, and three to four weeks apart seems to be optimal. Each vaccine usually consists of several different viruses (e.g., parvovirus, distemper, parainfluenza, hepatitis) combined into one injection. Coronavirus can be given as a separate vaccination according to this same schedule if pups are at risk. Some veterinarians and breeders advise another parvovirus booster at 18–20

weeks of age. A booster is given for all vaccines at one year of age and annually thereafter. For animals at increased risk of exposure, parvovirus vaccination may be given as often as four times a year. A new vaccine for canine cough (tracheo-bronchitis) is squirted into the nostrils. It can be given as early as six weeks of age if pups are at risk. Leptospirosis vaccination is given in some geographic areas and likely offers protection for six to eight months. The initial series consists of three to four injections spaced three to four weeks apart, starting as early as ten weeks of age. Rabies vaccine is given as a separate injection at three months of age, repeated when the pup is one year old, then repeated every one to three years depending on local risk and government regulation.

Between 8 and 14 weeks of age, use every opportunity to expose the pup to as many people and situations as possible. This is part of the critical socialization period that will determine how good a pet your dog will become. This is not the time to abandon a puppy for eight hours while you go to work. This is also not the time to punish your dog in any way, shape, or form.

This is the time to introduce

your dog to neighborhood cats, birds, and other creatures. Hold off on exposure to other dogs until after the second vaccination in the series. You don't want your new friend to pick up contagious diseases from other dogs before it has adequate protec- situation it is likely to encounter in its life. Take it in cars, elevators, buses, travel crates, subways, to parade grounds, parks, beaches; you want it to habituate to all environments. Expose your pup to kids, teenagers, old people, people in wheelchairs,

A group of eight-week-old Yorkie pups. At this age puppies are ready to go to their new homes and should already have at least one set of inoculations.

tion. By 12 weeks of age, your pup should be ready for social outings with other dogs. Do it— it's a great way for your dog to feel comfortable around members of its own species. Walk the streets and introduce your pup to everybody you meet. Your goal should be to introduce your dog to every type of person or people on bicycles, people in uniforms. The more varied the exposure, the better the socialization.

Proper identification of your pet is also important since this minimizes the risk of theft and increases the chances that your pet will be returned to you if it is lost. There are several different options. Microchip implantation is a relatively painless procedure involving the subcutaneous injection of an implant the size of a grain of rice. This implant does not act as a beacon if your pet is missing. However, if your pet turns up at a veterinary clinic or shelter and is checked with a scanner, the chip provides information about the owner that can be used to quickly reunite you with your pet. This method of identification is reasonably priced, permanent in nature, and performed at most veterinary clinics. Another option is tattooing, which can be done on the inner ear or on the skin of the abdomen. Most purebreds are given a number by the associated registry (e.g., American Kennel Club, United Kennel Club, Canadian Kennel Club, etc.) and this is used for identification, or permanent numbers such as social security numbers (telephone numbers and addresses may change during the life of your pet) can be used in the tattooing process. There are several different tattoo registries maintaining lists of dogs, their tattoo codes, and their owners. Finally, identification tags and collars provide quick information but can be separated from your pet if it is lost or stolen. They work best when combined

with a permanent identification system such as microchip implantation or tattooing.

FOUR TO TWELVE MONTHS OF AGE

At 16 weeks of age, when your pup gets the last in its series of regular induction vaccinations, ask your veterinarian about evaluating the pup for hip dysplasia with the PennHip™ technique. This helps predict the dog's risk of developing hip dysplasia as well as degenerative joint disease. Yorkshire Terrier breeders have done an excellent job decreasing the incidence of hip dysplasia through routine screening and registration programs. Since anesthesia is typically required for the procedure, many veterinarians like to do the evaluation at the same time as neutering. Since the incidence of hip dysplasia is so low in Yorkshire Terriers, many veterinarians only recommend that breeding animals be checked at this time.

At this time, it is very worthwhile to perform a diagnostic test for von Willebrand's disease, an inherited disorder that causes uncontrolled bleeding. A simple blood test is all that is required, but it may need to be sent to a special laboratory to have the test performed. You will be extremely happy that you had the foresight to have this done before neutering. If your dog does have a bleeding problem, it will be necessary to take special precautions during surgery.

As a general rule, neuter your animal at about six months of age unless you fully intend to breed it. As we know, neutering can be safely done at eight weeks of age but this is still not a common practice. Neutering not only stops the possibility of pregnancy and undesirable behaviors but can prevent several health problems as well. It is a well-established fact that female pups spayed before their first heat have a dramatically reduced incidence of mammary (breast) cancer. Neutered males significantly decrease their incidence of prostate disorders.

Also when your pet is six months of age, your veterinarian will want to take a blood sample to perform a heartworm test. If the test is negative and shows no evidence of heartworm infection, the pup will start heartworm prevention therapy. Some veterinarians are even rec-

By the time your Yorkshire Terrier is one year of age, he should be accustomed to wearing a leash and collar. Owner, Leroy M. Chavez.

ommending preventive therapy in younger pups. This might be a once-a-day regimen, but newer therapies can be given on a once-a-month basis. As a bonus, most of these heartworm preventatives also help prevent internal parasites.

Another part of the six-month visit should be a thorough dental evaluation to make sure all the permanent teeth have correctly erupted. If they haven't, this will be the time to correct the problem. Correction should only be performed to make the animal more comfortable and to promote normal chewing. The procedures should never be used to cosmetically improve the appearance of a dog used for show purposes or breeding.

After the dental evaluation, you should start implementing home dental care. In most cases, this will consist of brushing the teeth one or more times each week and perhaps using dental rinses. It is a sad fact that 85% of dogs over four years of age have periodontal disease and "doggy breath." In fact, it is so common that most people think it is "normal." Well, it is normal—as normal as bad breath would be in people if they never brushed

A thorough dental evaluation should be given when your Yorkie is six months old to ensure that all the adult teeth have come in properly.

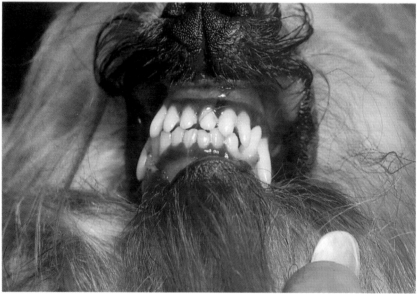

Provide your teething Yorkshire Terrier puppy with Gumabones®. They are made from polyurethane and are best for young puppies due to their softer composition.

their teeth. Brush your dog's teeth regularly with a special toothbrush and toothpaste and you can greatly reduce the incidence of tartar buildup, bad breath, and gum disease. Provide the Puppy Bone™ from Nylabone® and a Gumabone® to puppies as early as eight to ten weeks. Nylabones® not only help in the proper development of the puppy's jaw and the emergence of adult teeth but help to keep the teeth clean...and the breath fresh. Better preventive care means that dogs live longer. They'll enjoy their sunset years more if they still have

their teeth. Ask your veterinarian for details on home dental care.

ONE TO SEVEN YEARS OF AGE

At one year of age, your dog should be re-examined and have boosters for all vaccines. Your veterinarian will also want to do a very thorough physical examination to look for early evidence of problems. This might include taking radiographs (x-rays) of the hips and elbows to look for evidence of dysplastic changes. Genetic Disease Control (GDC) will certify hips and

When the adult Yorkshire Terrier coat is fully grown in, it should be glossy, fine, and silky in texture, with the proper blue and tan markings. Color and richness of tan on the head and legs are of prime importance.

elbows at 12 months of age; the Orthopedic Foundation for Animals won't issue certification until 24 months of age.

At 12 months of age, it's also a great time to have some blood samples analyzed to provide background information. Although few Yorkshire Terriers experience clinical problems at this young age, troubles may be starting. Therefore, it is a good idea to have baseline levels of thyroid hormones (free and total), blood cell counts, organ chemistries, and cholesterol levels. This can serve as a valuable comparison to samples collected in the future.

Each year, preferably around the time of your pet's birthday, it's time for another veterinary visit. This visit is a wonderful opportunity for a thorough clinical examination rather than just "shots." Since 85% of dogs have periodontal disease by four years of age, veterinary intervention does not seem to be as widespread as it should be. The examination should include visually inspecting the ears, eyes (a great time to start scrutinizing for progressive retinal atrophy, cataracts, etc.), mouth (don't wait for gum disease), and groin, listening (auscultation) to the lungs and heart, feeling (palpating) the lymph nodes and abdomen, and answering all of your questions about optimal health care. In addition, booster vaccinations are given during these times, stool samples are checked for parasites, urine is analyzed, and blood samples may be collected for analysis. One of the tests run on the blood samples is for heartworm antigen. In areas of the country where heartworm is only present in the spring, summer, and fall (it's spread by mosquitoes), blood samples are collected and evaluated about a month prior to the mosquito season. Other routine blood tests are for blood cells (hematology), organ chemistries, thyroid levels, and electrolytes.

By two years of age, most veterinarians prefer to begin preventive dental cleanings, often referred to as "prophies." Anesthesia is required and the veterinarian or veterinary dentist will use an ultrasonic scaler to remove plaque and tartar from above and below the gum line and polish the teeth so that plaque has a harder time sticking to the teeth. Radiographs (x-rays) and fluoride treatments are other options. It is now known that it is plaque, not tartar, that initiates inflammation in the gums. Since scaling and root planing remove

Be sure that your Yorkshire Terrier always has safe chew toys, like a Gumabone® or a Gumadisc®.

more tartar than plaque, veterinary dentists have begun using a new technique called PerioBUD (Periodontal Bactericidal Ultrasonic Debridement). The ultrasonic treatment is quicker, disrupts more bacteria, and is less irritating to the gums. With tooth polishing to finish up the procedure, gum healing is better and owners can start home care sooner. Each dog has its own dental needs that must be addressed, but most veterinary dentists recommend prophies annually. Be sure too that your Yorkshire Terrier always has a Nylabone® available to do his part in keeping his teeth clean.

SENIOR YORKSHIRE TERRIERS

Yorkshire Terriers are considered seniors when they reach about seven years of age. Veterinarians still usually only need to examine them once a year, but it is now important to start screening for geriatric problems. Accordingly blood profiles, urinalysis, chest radiographs (x-rays), and electrocardiograms (EKGs) are recommended on an annual basis. When problems are caught early, they are much more likely to be successfully managed. This is as true in canine medicine as it is in human medicine.

MEDICAL PROBLEMS

**RECOGNIZED GENETIC CONDITIONS
SPECIFICALLY RELATED TO THE YORKSHIRE TERRIER**

Many conditions appear to be especially prominent in Yorkshire Terriers. Sometimes it is possible to identify the genetic basis of a problem, but in many cases, we must be satisfied with merely identifying the breeds that are at risk and how the conditions can be identified, treated, and prevented.

Facing page: Eyes, ears, and elbows—your veterinarian should thoroughly evaluate your Yorkshire Terrier. All Yorkies, whether intended for breeding or not, need to be screened for potentially debilitating conditions.

Following are some conditions that have been recognized as being common in the Yorkshire Terrier but this listing is certainly not complete. Also, many genetic conditions may be common in certain breed lines, but not in the breed in general.

CATARACTS

Cataracts refer to an opacity or cloudiness on the lens and ophthalmologists are careful to categorize them on the basis of stage, age of onset, and location. In Yorkshire Terriers, the genetic basis and characterization of cataracts has not yet been completely defined. The cataracts are usually evident between three and six years of age. Many dogs adapt well to cataracts, but cataract removal surgery is available and quite successful if needed. The condition may be associated with persistent hyperplastic primary vitreous as discussed below. Affected animals and their siblings should obviously not be used for breeding and careful ophthalmologic evaluation of both parents is warranted.

COLLAPSED TRACHEA

Collapsed trachea is a flattening in the upper portion of the trachea that results in a dry "honking" cough and occasional difficulty breathing, eating, and drinking. The condition is known to run in families but a genetic basis has only been postulated. Others have suggested that diet, obesity, infection, and neurological abnormalities may play a role. As a general rule, it occurs most often in middle-aged, obese small breeds of dogs, including Yorkshire Terriers, Toy Poodles, Pomeranians, and Chihuahuas. Diagnosis is not usually difficult and the "honking" characteristic is a very telling sign. Other important tests are radiographs (x-rays) taken while the animal breathes in and out. A tracheal wash and tracheoscopy are also very helpful in determining exactly what is going on in any individual case.

In most cases, medical management is sufficient to control the problem. Weight loss is mandatory and this relieves much pressure on the respiratory system. A harness is substituted for a collar. Training is instituted so that affected dogs don't respond to things by getting excited. Stress tends to bring on "attacks." Antibiotics are used if infections (e.g., canine cough, bronchitis, tracheitis) are components of the problem. Steam vaporizer therapy may also be

Your Yorkie's eyes should be sparkling and dark in color. Any persisting cloudiness or opacity on the lens should be checked by a veterinarian.

useful and there are a variety of medications available to dilate the bronchi and suppress the cough if your veterinarian feels they are necessary. Finally, as a last resort, there are surgical approaches to the problem if all else fails. Affected individuals should not be used in breeding programs.

CRYPTORCHIDISM

Cryptorchidism refers to testicles that have not descended into the scrotum. During fetal development, the testicles migrate from within the abdomen through an opening into the scrotum. In some cases, however, the transition is incomplete and one or both testicles remain within the abdomen. It is believed to be at least partially a hereditary condition. The actual cause is still a matter of some debate, but it is thought that insufficient stimulation of sex organs during fetal development may be partially to blame. Dogs that are cryptorchid have a much higher incidence of testicular cancer and are not suitable for show purposes.

The diagnosis is easily made but pups are generally given

until four months of age before the testicles are expected to be fully descended. Dogs that are cryptorchid should be neutered for two reasons. First, they shouldn't be bred and possibly pass along the trait. Second, they have an increased incidence of testicular cancer if neutering isn't done.

ELBOW DYSPLASIA

Elbow dysplasia doesn't refer to just one disease, but rather an entire range of disorders that affect the elbow joint. Elbow dysplasia and osteochondrosis are disorders of young dogs, with problems usually starting between four and seven months of age. The usual manifestation is a sudden onset of lameness. In time, the continued inflammation results in arthritis in those affected joints.

Yorkshire Terriers are not particularly prone to elbow dysplasia. However, since the incidence is so low, continued registration of breeding animals is recommended because it should be possible to completely eliminate the condition in Yorkshire Terriers by conscientious breeding.

Radiographs (x-rays) are taken of the elbow joints and submitted to a registry for evaluation. The Orthopedic Foundation for Animals (OFA) will assign a breed registry number to those animals with normal elbows that are over 24 months of age. Abnormal elbows are reported as Grade I to III, where Grade III elbows have well-developed degenerative joint disease (arthritis). Normal elbows on individuals 24 months or older are assigned a breed registry number and are periodically reported to parent breed clubs. Genetic Disease Control (GDC) maintains an open registry for elbow dysplasia and assigns a registry number to those individuals with normal elbows at 12 months of age or older. Only animals with "normal" elbows should be used for breeding.

HIP DYSPLASIA

Hip dysplasia is a genetically transmitted developmental problem of the hip joint that is common in many breeds. Fortunately, it is relatively rare in the Yorkshire Terrier. Dogs may be born with a "susceptibility" or "tendency" to develop hip dysplasia but it is not a foregone conclusion that all susceptible dogs will eventually develop hip dysplasia. All dysplastic dogs are born with normal hips and the dysplastic changes begin within the first 24 months of life, although they are usually evident long before then.

When purchasing a Yorkshire Terrier pup, it is best to ensure that the parents were both registered with normal hips through one of the international registries such as the Orthopedic Foundation for Animals or Genetic Disease Control. Pups over 16 weeks of age can be tested by veterinarians trained in the PennHip™ procedure, which is a way of predicting a dog's risk of developing hip dysplasia and arthritis. In time it should be possible to completely eradicate hip dysplasia from the breed.

HYPOTHYROIDISM

Hypothyroidism is the most commonly diagnosed endocrine (hormonal) problem in the Yorkshire Terrier. The disease itself refers to an insufficient amount of thyroid hormones being produced. Although there are several different potential causes, lymphocytic thyroiditis is by far the most common. Iodine deficiency and goiter are extremely rare. In lymphocytic thyroiditis, the body produces antibodies that target aspects of thyroid tissue; the process usually starts between one and three years of age in affected animals but doesn't become

clinically evident until later in life.

There is a great deal of misinformation about hypothyroidism. Owners often expect affected dogs to be obese with the condition and otherwise don't suspect it. The fact is that hypothyroidism is quite variable in its manifestations and obesity is only seen in a small percentage of cases. In most cases, affected animals appear fine until they use up most of their remaining thyroid hormone reserves. The most common manifestations, then, are lack of energy and recurrent infections. Hair loss is seen in about one-third of cases.

You might suspect that hypothyroidism would be easy to diagnose but it is trickier than you may think. Since there is a large reserve of thyroid hormones in the body, a test measuring only total blood levels of the hormones (T-4 and T-3) is not a very sensitive indicator of the condition. Thyroid stimulation tests are the best way to measure the functional reserve. Measuring "free" and "total" levels of the hormones and/or endogenous TSH (thyroid-stimulating hormone) are other approaches. Also, since we know that most cases are due to antibodies produced in the body, screening for these autoantibodies can help identify animals at risk of developing hypothyroidism.

Periodic "screening" for the disorder is warranted in many cases. Although none of the screening tests are perfect, a

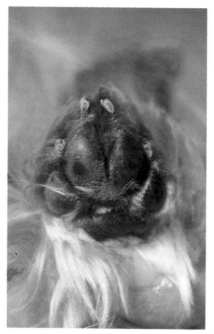

Check your Yorkie's paws regularly; the pads should be black. Any signs of excessive licking or chewing may be an indication of an allergy or some other problem.

basic panel evaluating total T-4, free T-4, TSH, and cholesterol levels is a good start. Ideally, this would first be performed at one year of age and annually

thereafter. This "screening" is practical, because none of these tests is very expensive.

Fortunately, although there may be some problems in diagnosing hypothyroidism, treatment is straightforward and relatively inexpensive. Supplementing the affected animal twice daily with thyroid hormone effectively treats the condition. In many breeds, supplementation with thyroid hormones is commonly done to help confirm the diagnosis. Animals with hypothyroidism should not be used in a breeding program and those with circulating autoantibodies but no actual hypothyroid disease should also not be used for breeding.

INHALANT ALLERGIES

Inhalant allergy is the canine version of hay fever and is extremely common. Whereas people with allergies often sneeze, dogs with allergies scratch—they're itchy. The most common manifestations include licking and chewing at the front feet. There may also be face rubbing, a rash on the belly or in the armpits, and subsequent bacterial infections on the skin surface. The offenders are molds, pollens, and house dust that are present in the air. Most dogs start to have problems some time after six months of age.

Allergies are diagnosed in dogs similar to the way they are diagnosed in people. Intradermal (skin) testing is the most specific test and is usually done by veterinary dermatologists or others in referral settings. Blood tests are also available for allergy testing but are, at present, less reliable.

Mild cases of allergy can be treated with antihistamines, fatty acid supplements (combinations of eicosapentaenoic acid and gamma-linolenic acid), and frequent soothing baths. Allergies that last for more than three to four months each year or are severe are best treated with immunotherapy (allergy shots). Corticosteroids effectively reduce the itch of allergy but can cause other medical problems with long-term use. One of the quickest ways to comfort an allergic pet is with a relaxing bath. The effect doesn't last long, but it does help to relieve itchiness. The bath water should be cool rather than

Mild cases of allergy can be treated with frequent soothing baths, using any of a variety of medicated shampoos available from your veterinarian.

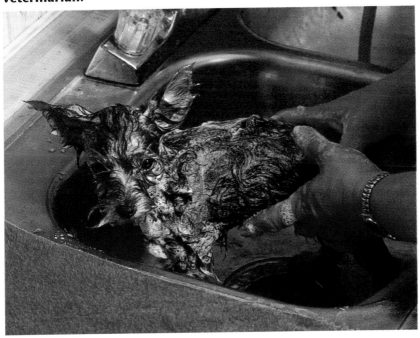

hot since hot water can actually make the itchiness worse. Adding colloidal oatmeal powder or Epsom salts to the bath water makes it even more soothing and a variety of medicated shampoos available from veterinarians will also improve the situation. It is unlikely that a medicated bath will reduce itchiness for more than a couple of days but it is a safe way to give your allergic pet some relief and it can be repeated frequently. Some newer forms of allergy shampoos even incorporate safe corticosteroids that help provide symptomatic relief of itching. There are many safe sprays available from your veterinarian that can also give some temporary relief. If the allergies are complicated by infection, the infection may also be itchy; antibiotics are sometimes required.

The only effective way of preventing inhalant allergies is to select pups from parents that aren't allergic themselves. This is a complicated process since animals may be bred before they are old enough to show evidence of allergies.

KERATOCONJUNCTIVITIS SICCA

Keratoconjunctivitis sicca (KCS) or "dry eye" is a common condition seen in dogs and many breeds are prone, including the Yorkshire Terrier. It results from reduction in the amount of tears produced by the lacrimal (tear) glands. While some cases are congenital, many result from infections, underlying problems, and immunological diseases. With KCS, the lack of tears causes dry areas on the corneal surface, which then cause damage. You can't tell by looking that there are not enough tears, but often you can see an accumulation of mucus in and around the eye. In time, the cornea becomes cloudy and vision is impaired. Diagnosis is relatively easy since tear production can be measured simply with a Schirmer tear test. A thin strip of paper is placed inside the lower eyelid for one minute and the tears that it absorbs can be measured to determine whether or not tear production is normal. Rheumatoid Factor and Antinuclear Antibody (ANA) tests are typically run to determine which cases may have an immunologic component.

Treatment should be immediate to prevent further damage to the cornea. Antibiotics are often necessary because infection tends to accompany the condition. Artificial tears are used several times a day to replenish the tear film. For immunologically-induced KCS, the drug cyclosporine can be very successful. The drug pilocarpine is also sometimes dispensed to be added to the food. Success is inconsistent. For those animals that do not respond to medical therapy and have normal saliva production, there is a surgical option called parotid duct transposition. Animals with congenital or immunologic KCS should not be used in breeding programs.

LEGG-CALVE-PERTHES DISEASE

Legg-Calve-Perthes disease is a disorder of the hip joint seen in young, small-breed dogs. It is also known as aseptic necrosis of the femoral head. The Yorkshire Terrier appears to be particularly prone. It is most commonly seen in dogs between 4 and 12 months of age. The exact cause is unknown but only one leg is involved in the majority (85%) of cases. A genetic trend (autosomal recessive with incomplete penetrance) has been suggested.

Affected dogs are usually lame and often experience pain when the leg is moved or manipulated. There is often substantial atrophy of muscle in the affected area. Once again, this tends to be a disease of young dogs, most being under a year of age when the problem was first detected.

The diagnosis can be strongly suspected on the basis of radiographic studies, and is confirmed by surgical biopsies. For some unknown reason, the bone of the femoral head just dies (avascular necrosis) and collapses in upon itself. The Institute for Genetic Disease Control in Animals (GDC) plans to provide a registry for this condition in the near future. The time-honored treatment for this condition is surgical removal of the femoral head (femoral head ostectomy). This is because there is little chance that the problem will resolve itself. Affected animals, their siblings, and their parents should be removed from any breeding programs.

MEDIAL PATELLAR LUXATION

The patella is the kneecap and patellar luxation refers to the condition when the kneecap slips out of its usual resting place and lodges on the inside (medial aspect) of the knee. It is a congenital problem of dogs but the degree of patellar displacement may increase with time as the tissues stretch and the bones continue to deform.

The condition is seen primarily in small and toy breeds of dog.

Medial patellar luxation may be graded by veterinarians as to how much laxity there is in the patella. No laxity is preferred and affected individuals may have Grade 1 (mild) through Grade IV (severe). The diagnosis can be made by manipulating the knee joint to see if the kneecap luxates towards the inner (medial) aspect of the leg. There is usually little or no pain associated with this process. Radiography (x-rays) can be used to document persistent luxation and to evaluate for other abnormalities such as arthritic changes.

Older dogs and those mildly affected may respond to conservative therapy, but surgery is often recommended for young dogs before arthritic changes become evident. There are several successful surgical techniques for this condition. After surgery, dogs should have enforced rest for six weeks while healing, and leash activity only. The results are excellent in most cases.

The best form of prevention is to only purchase animals that have no family history of medial patellar luxation. Registries are maintained by the Orthopedic Foundation for Animals (OFA) and the Institute for Genetic Disease Control in Animals (GDC).

PROGRESSIVE RETINAL ATROPHY

Progressive retinal atrophy (PRA) refers to several inherited disorders affecting the retina that result in blindness. PRA is thought to be inherited, with each breed demonstrating a specific age of onset and pattern of inheritance. The disease gene for PRA in the Yorkshire Terrier has not yet been defined, but the onset is typically very late in this breed, usually 5–11 years of age. There is progressive atrophy or degeneration of the retinal tissue. Visual impairment occurs slowly but progressively. Therefore, animals often adapt to their reduced vision until it is compromised to near blindness. Because of this, owners may not notice any visual impairment until the condition has progressed significantly.

The diagnosis of PRA can be made in two ways: direct visualization of the retina and electroretinography (ERG). The use of indirect ophthalmoscopy requires a great deal of training and expertise and is more commonly performed by ophthalmology specialists than general practitioners. The other is a highly sensitive test, usually available only from specialists, electroretinography. The procedure is painless, but usually available only from specialty centers. This instrument is sensitive enough to detect even the early onset of disease. Unfortunately there is no treatment available for progressive reti-

gist. The best guarantee is to buy pups from a source that regularly screens their breeding animals and has them registered with CERF. A DNA-based blood test has now been developed that detects normals, affected animals, and carriers of the Irish Setter breed. Additional research should eventually pro-

There are many conditions that can affect the eyes of your Yorkshire Terrier. Breeding animals should be examined annually by a veterinary ophthalmologist.

nal atrophy and all affected dogs eventually go blind. Identification of affected breeding animals is essential to prevent spread of the condition within the breed. Breeding animals should be examined annually by a veterinary ophthalmolo-

duce a test suitable for the Yorkshire Terrier.

ULCERATIVE KERATITIS

Ulcerative keratitis refers to the formation of ulcers on the surface of the cornea. Because the Yorkie has fur that often brushes its eyes, the cornea is prone to a variety of insults, including infection, trauma, and exposure to eyelashes, fur, dust, dirt, and toxins. The resultant ulcer can be superficial or deep enough to puncture the eye.

The clinical signs (symptoms) associated with ulcerative keratitis are blinking, pain, watering (epiphora), and general discomfort. The extent of the defect is determined by careful examination of the eyes and the application of Fluoroscein or Rose Bengal stains. These tend to outline the defects but not necessarily determine the depth of penetration.

There are a variety of ways of treating corneal ulcers depending on how deep they are. Medical therapy with antibiotics, artificial tears, and atropine are adequate in mild cases. More chronic or recurrent ulcers require contact lenses, collagen patches, or surgical intervention. There are a variety of surgical approaches to treat chronic or recurrent ulcers. Ulcerative keratitis does not appear to be inherited. It seems to be a function of having large eyes in a small, long-haired dog.

VALVULAR INSUFFICIENCY

Valvular insufficiency occurs when the valves between the different chambers of the heart fail to maintain a tight seal. The most common form, mitral insufficiency, is thought to run in families of dogs. In many cases, the condition poses no problems, or not until the animal reaches middle age. The most characteristic finding in this early stage is a heart murmur, which is usually easy to detect. In later stages, when heart function has been compromised, the problems will be evident on radiographs (x-rays) and echocardiograms. Electrocardiograms (EKGs) do not usually detect problems until the condition is quite advanced. Treatment is more difficult in dogs because valve replacement surgery is not routinely performed in animals. Highly-stressed animals may be given tranquilizers such as phenobarbital or diazepam to help prevent further degeneration of the valves. Eventually, treatment will be instituted for heart failure, including drugs such as isosorbide dinitrate, diuretics (water pills), and Angiotensin-converting enzyme (ACE) inhibitors. Until the genetics of valvular insufficiency are better understood, dogs with even mild forms of mitral insufficiency should not be used for breeding.

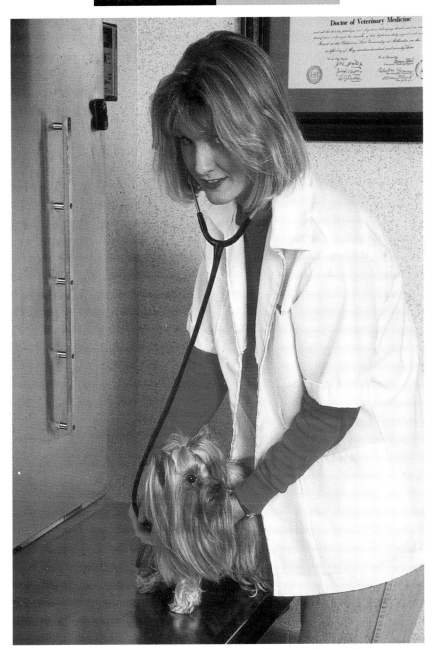

Valvular insufficiency is a recognized condition in Yorkshire Terriers. It can be easily detected by a heart murmur.

VERTEBRAL MALFORMATION

Vertebral malformation refers to a malalignment or instability of the spine. As a consequence, affected dogs can suffer from compression of the spinal cord. The exact cause is unknown, but it does run in families, at least in Yorkshire Terriers and English Bulldogs. In many cases there are no problems at all. In others, the malalignment ends up compressing the spinal cord and causing weakness and difficulty walking. In most cases where the problems are going to be clinical, the problem is evident at less than one year of age. The diagnosis can be confirmed in many cases with radiographs (x-rays), but sometimes it is necessary to inject a dye into the spinal cord to outline the defect (myelography). The only treatment to permanently control the situation is surgery. Affected animals should not be used for breeding. Be aware, however, that many animals have mild cases of vertebral malformation that cause no problems. Therefore, if one of your pets develops vertebral malformation, it is impossible to dismiss the parents as normal just because they haven't experienced problems themselves.

VON WILLEBRAND'S DISEASE

Von Willebrand's disease (vWD) is the most common inherited bleeding disorder of dogs. The abnormal gene can be inherited from one or both parents. If both parents pass on the gene, most of the resultant pups fail to thrive and most will die. In most cases, though, the pup inherits a relative lack of clotting ability that is quite variable. For instance, one dog may have 15% of the clotting factor, while another might have 60%. The higher the amount, the less likely it will be that the bleeding will be readily evident since spontaneous bleeding is usually only seen when dogs have less than 30% of the normal level of von Willebrand clotting factor. Thus, some dogs don't get diagnosed until they are neutered or spayed and they end up bleeding uncontrollably or they develop pockets of blood (hematomas) at the surgical site. In addition to the inherited form of vWD, this disorder can also be acquired in association with familial hypothyroidism. This form is usually seen in Yorkshire Terriers older than five years of age.

Von Willebrand's disease is extremely important in the Yorkshire Terrier because the incidence appears to be on the rise.

However, there is good news. There are tests available to determine the amount of von Willebrand factor in the blood and they are accurate and reasonably priced. Yorkshire Terriers used for breeding should have normal amounts of von Willebrand factor in their blood and so should all pups that are adopted as household pets. Carriers should not be used for breeding, even if they appear clinically normal. Since hypothyroidism can be linked with von Willebrand's disease, thyroid profiles can also be a useful part of the screening procedure in older Yorkshire Terriers.

OTHER CONDITIONS COMMONLY SEEN IN THE YORKSHIRE TERRIER

- Distichiasis
- Entropion
- Hydrocephalus
- Hypoglycemia
- Open Fontanels
- Persistent Pupillary Membranes
- Portosystemic Shunt
- Retained Primary Teeth
- Retinal Detachment
- Retinal Dysplasia
- Short-Hair Syndrome
- Subepithelial Geographic Cornea

To ensure the good health of future generations of the breed, all Yorkshire Terriers used for breeding should be carefully screened for hereditary diseases.

INFECTIONS & INFESTATIONS

**HOW TO PROTECT YOUR YORKSHIRE TERRIER
FROM PARASITES AND MICROBES**

An important part of keeping your Yorkshire Terrier healthy is to prevent problems caused by parasites and microbes. Although there are a variety of drugs available that can help limit problems, prevention is always the desired option. Taking the proper precautions leads to less aggravation, less itching, and less expense.

Facing Page: Problems caused by parasites and microbes can drive your Yorkshire Terrier batty; take the proper precautions to control these scary little critters.

FLEAS

Fleas are common parasites but not an inevitable part of every pet-owner's reality. If you take the time to understand some of the basics of flea population dynamics, control is both conceivable and practical.

Fleas have four life stages (egg, larva, pupa, adult) and each stage responds to some therapies while being resistant to others. Failing to understand this is the major reason why some people have so much trouble getting the upper hand in the battle to control fleas.

Fleas spend all their time on dogs and only leave if physically removed by brushing, bathing, or scratching. However, the eggs that are laid on the animal are not sticky and fall to the ground, contaminating the environment. Our goal must be to remove fleas from the animals in the house, from the house itself, and from the immediate outdoor environment. Part of our plan must also involve using different medications to get rid of the different life stages as well as minimizing the use of potentially harmful insecticides that could be poisonous for pets and family members.

A flea comb is a very handy device for recovering fleas from pets. The best places to comb are the tailhead, groin area, armpits, back, and neck region. Collected fleas should be dropped into a container of alcohol, which quickly kills them before they can escape. In addition, all pets should be bathed with a cleansing shampoo or flea shampoo to remove fleas and eggs. This has no residual effect, however, and fleas can jump back on immediately after the bath if nothing else is done. Rather than using potent insecticidal dips and sprays, consider products containing safe pyrethrins, imidacloprid or fipronil, and insect growth regulators (such as methoprene and pyripoxyfen) or insect development inhibitors (IDIs) such as lufenuron. These products are not only extremely safe, but the combination is effective against eggs, larvae, and adults. This only leaves the pupal stage to cause continued problems. Insect growth regulators can also be safely given as once-a-month oral preparations. Flea collars are rarely useful, and electronic flea collars are not to be recommended for any dogs.

To clean up the household, vacuuming is a good first step because it picks up about 50% of the flea eggs and it also stimulates flea pupae to emerge as adults, a stage when they are easier to kill with insecticides. The vacuum bag should be removed and discarded with each treatment. Household treatment can then be initiated with pyrethrins and a combination of either insect growth regulators or sodium polyborate (a borax derivative). The pyrethrins need to be reapplied every two to three weeks but the insect growth regulators last about two to three months and many companies guarantee sodium polyborate for a full year. Stronger insecticides such as carbamates and organophosphates can be used and will last three to four weeks in the household, but they are potentially toxic and offer no real advantages other than their persistence in the home environment. This is also one of their major disadvantages.

When an insecticide is combined with an insect growth regulator, flea control is most likely to be successful. The insecticide kills the adult fleas and the insect growth regulator affects the eggs and larvae. However, insecticides kill less than 20% of flea cocoons (pupae). Because of this, new fleas may hatch in two to three weeks despite appropriate application of products. This is known as the "pupal window" and is one of the most common obstacles to effective flea control. This is why a safe insecticide should be applied to the home environment two to three weeks after the initial treatment. This catches the newly hatched pupae before they have a chance to lay eggs and perpetuate the flea problem.

If treatment of the outdoor environment is needed, there are several options. Pyripoxyfen, an insect growth regulator, is stable in sunlight and can be used outdoors. Sodium polyborate can be used as well, but it is important that it not be inadvertently eaten by pets. Organophosphates and carbamates are sometimes recommended for outdoor use and it is not necessary to treat the entire property. Flea control should be directed predominantly at garden margins, porches, dog houses, garages, and other pet lounging areas. Fleas don't do well in direct exposure to sunlight so generalized lawn treatment is not needed. Finally, microscopic worms (nematodes) are available that can be sprayed onto the lawn with a garden sprayer. The nematodes eat immature flea forms and then biodegrade without harming anything else.

TICKS

Ticks are found world-wide and can cause a variety of problems including blood loss, tick paralysis, Lyme disease, "tick fever," Rocky Mountain Spotted Fever, and babesiosis. All are important diseases which need to be prevented whenever possible. This is only possible by limiting the exposure of our pets to ticks.

For those species of tick that dwell indoors, the eggs are laid mostly in cracks and on vertical surfaces in kennels and homes. Most other species are found outside in vegetation, such as grassy meadows, woods, brush, and weeds.

Ticks feed only on blood but they don't actually bite. They attach to a host by sticking their harpoon-shaped mouth-parts into the host's skin and sucking blood. Some ticks can increase their size 20—50 times as they feed. Favorite places for them to locate are between the toes and in the ears, although they can appear anywhere on the host's skin surface.

A good approach to preventing ticks is to remove underbrush and leaf litter, and to thin the trees in areas where dogs are allowed. This removes the cover and food sources for small mammals that serve as hosts for ticks. Ticks must have adequate cover that provides high levels of moisture and at the same time provides an opportunity for contact with animals. Keeping the lawn well maintained also makes ticks less likely to drop by and stay.

Because of the potential for ticks to transmit a variety of harmful diseases, dogs should be carefully inspected after walks through wooded areas (where ticks may be found) and any ticks should be removed carefully and promptly to prevent the spread of disease. Care should be taken not to squeeze, crush, or puncture the tick's body since exposure to the tick's body fluids may lead to the spread of any disease carried by that tick to the animal or to the person removing the tick. The tick should be disposed of in a container of alcohol or flushed down the toilet. If the site becomes infected, veterinary attention should be sought immediately. Insecticides and repellents should only be applied to pets following appropriate veterinary advice, since indiscriminate use can be dangerous. Recently, a new tick collar has become available that contains amitraz. This collar not only kills ticks but causes them to retract from the skin within two to three days. This greatly reduces the chances of ticks transmitting a variety of diseases. A spray formulation has also recently been developed and marketed. It might seem that there should be vac-

MANGE

Mange refers to any skin condition caused by mites. The contagious mites include ear mites, scabies mites, cheyletiella mites and chiggers. Demodectic mange is associated with prolif-

The best way to prevent ticks is to remove underbrush and leaf litter. This eliminates the cover and food source for small mammals that serve as hosts for ticks.

cines for all the diseases carried by ticks, but only a Lyme disease (*Borrelia burgdorferi*) vaccination is currently available.

eration of demodex mites but they are not considered contagious.

The most common causes of mange in dogs are ear mites

and these are extremely contagious. The best way to avoid ear mites is to buy pups from sources that don't have problems with ear mite infestation. Otherwise, pups readily acquire them when kept in crowded environments in which other animals might be carriers. Treatment is effective if whole body (or systemic) therapy is used, but relapses are common when medication in the ear canal is the only approach. This is because the mites tend to crawl out of the ear canal when medications are applied. They simply feed elsewhere on the body until it is safe for them to return to the ears.

Scabies mites and cheyletiella mites are passed on by other dogs that are carrying the mites. They are "social" diseases that can be prevented by avoiding exposure of your dog to others that are infested. Scabies (sarcoptic mange) has the dubious honor of being the most itchy disease to which dogs are susceptible. Chigger mites are present in forested areas and dogs acquire them by roaming in these areas. All types of mites can be effectively diagnosed and treated by your veterinarian should your dog happen to become infested.

HEARTWORM

Heartworm disease is caused by the worm *Dirofilaria immitis* and is spread by mosquitoes. The female heartworms produce microfilariae (baby worms) that circulate in the bloodstream, waiting to by picked up by mosquitoes to pass the infection along. Dogs do not get heartworm by socializing with infected dogs; they only get infected by mosquitoes that carry the infective microfilariae. The adult heartworms grow in the heart and major blood vessels and eventually cause heart failure.

Fortunately, heartworm is easily prevented by safe oral medications that can be administered daily or on a once-a-month basis. The once-a-month preparations also help prevent many of the common intestinal parasites, such as hookworms, roundworms, and whipworms.

Prior to giving any preventive medication for heartworm, an antigen test (an immunologic test that detects heartworms) should be performed by a veterinarian since it is dangerous to give the medication to dogs that harbor the parasite. Some experts also recommend a microfilarial test, just to be doubly certain. Once the test results show that the dog is free

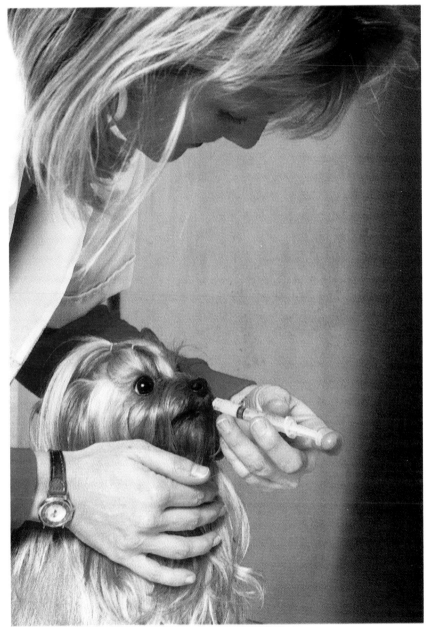

Heartworm, as well as other common intestinal parasites, can be prevented by safe oral medications that can be administered daily or on a once-a-month basis.

of heartworms, the preventive therapy can be commenced. The length of time the heartworm preventives must be given depends on the length of the mosquito season. In some parts of the country, dogs are on preventive therapy year round. Heartworm vaccines may soon be available but the preventives now available are easy to administer, inexpensive, and quite safe.

INTESTINAL PARASITES

The most important internal parasites in dogs are roundworms, hookworms, tapeworms, and whipworms. Roundworms are the most common. It has been estimated that 13 trillion roundworm eggs are discharged in dog feces every day! Studies have shown that 75% of all pups carry roundworms and start shedding them by three weeks of age. People are infected by exposure to dog feces containing infective roundworm eggs, not by handling pups. Hookworms can cause a disorder known as cutaneous larva migrans in people. In dogs, they are most dangerous to puppies since they latch onto the intestines and suck blood. They can cause anemia and even death when they are present in large numbers. The most common tapeworm is *Dipylidium caninum*, which is spread by fleas. However, another tapeworm (*Echinococcus multilocularis*) can cause fatal disease in people and can be spread to people from dogs. Whipworms live in the lower aspects of the intestines. Dogs get whipworms by consuming infective larvae. However, it may be another three months before they start shedding them in their stool, greatly complicating diagnosis. In other words, a dog can be infected by whipworms, but fecal evaluations are usually negative until the dog starts passing the eggs three months after becoming infected.

Other parasites, such as coccidia, cryptosporidium, giardia, and flukes can also cause problems in dogs. The best way to prevent all internal parasite problems is to have pups dewormed according to your veterinarian's recommendations, and to have parasite checks done on a regular basis, at least annually.

VIRAL INFECTIONS

Dogs get viral infections such as distemper, hepatitis, parvovirus, and rabies by exposure to infected animals. The key to prevention is controlled exposure to other animals and, of course, vaccination. Today's vaccines are extremely effective and properly vaccinated dogs are at minimal risk for contracting these diseases. However, it is still important to limit your dog's exposure to other animals that might be harboring infection. When selecting a facility for boarding or grooming, make sure the facility limits its clientele to animals that have documented vaccine histories. This is in everyone's best interest. Similarly, make sure your veterinarian has a quarantine area for infected dogs and that animals aren't admitted for surgery, boarding, grooming, or diagnostic testing without up-to-date vaccinations. By controlling exposure and ensuring vaccination, your pet should be safe from these potentially devastating diseases.

It is beyond the scope of this book to settle all the controversies of vaccination but they are worth mentioning. Should vaccines be combined in a single injection? It's convenient and cheaper to do it this way, but might some vaccine ingredients interfere with others? Some say yes, some say no. Are vaccine schedules designed for convenience or effectiveness? Mostly convenience. Some ingredients may only need to be given every two or more years but research

Today's vaccines are extremely effective and properly vaccinated dogs are at minimal risk of contracting viral infections.

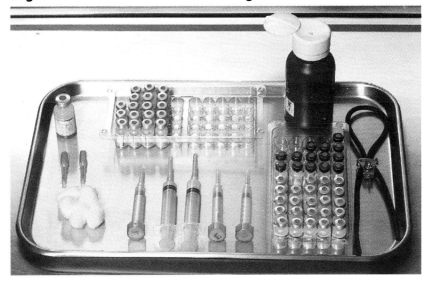

is incomplete. Should the dose of the vaccine vary with weight or should a Yorkshire Terrier receive the same dose as a Great Dane? Good questions, no definitive answers. Finally, should we be using modified-live or inactivated vaccine products? There is no short answer for this debate. Ask your veterinarian and do a lot of reading yourself!

CANINE COUGH

Canine infectious tracheo–bronchitis, also known as canine cough and kennel cough, is a contagious viral/bacterial disease that results in a hacking cough that may persist for many weeks. It is common wherever dogs are kept in close quarters, such as kennels, grooming parlors, dog shows, training classes, and even veterinary clinics. The condition doesn't respond well to most medications, but eventually clears spontaneously over the course of many weeks. Pneumonia is a possible but uncommon complication.

Limit your dog's exposure to other dogs and make sure that any dog he comes in contact with has been properly vaccinated.

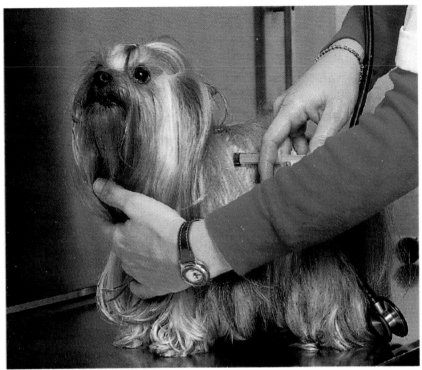

Preventing canine cough is best achieved by having your dog vaccinated. In order to ensure maximum protection, avoid contact with other animals for at least two weeks following the vaccination.

Prevention is best achieved by limiting exposure and having your dog vaccinated. The fewer opportunities you give your dog to come in contact with others, the less the likelihood of getting infected. Vaccination is not foolproof because many different viruses can be involved. Parainfluenza virus is included in most vaccines and is one of the more common viruses known to initiate the condition. *Bordetella bronchiseptica* is the bacterium most often associated with tracheobronchitis and a vaccine is now available that needs to be repeated twice yearly for dogs at risk. This vaccine is squirted into the nostrils to help stop the infection before it gets deeper into the respiratory tract. Make sure the vaccination is given several days (preferably two weeks) before exposure to ensure maximum protection.

FIRST AID

by Judy Iby, RVT

KNOWING YOUR DOG IN GOOD HEALTH

With some experience, you will learn how to give your dog a physical at home, and consequently will learn to recognize many potential problems.

If you can detect a problem early, you can seek timely medical help and thereby decrease your dog's risk of developing a more serious problem.

Facing page: There are many dangers in the home, as well as outside the home, that your Yorkshire Terrier may encounter. Therefore, it is important to know how to administer first aid in these situations.

Every pet owner should be able to take his pet's temperature, pulse, respirations, and check the capillary refill time (CRT). Knowing what is normal will alert the pet owner to what is abnormal, and this can be life saving for the sick pet.

TEMPERATURE

The dog's normal temperature is 100.5 to 102.5 degrees Fahrenheit. Take the temperature rectally for at least one minute. Be sure to shake the thermometer down first, and you may find it helpful to lubri-

It is easy to take your Yorkshire Terrier's temperature with the dog in a standing position. Be sure to hold the thermometer so it isn't expelled or sucked in.

cate the end. It is easy to take the temperature with the dog in a standing position. Be sure to hold on to the thermometer so that it isn't expelled or sucked in. A dog could have an elevated temperature if he is excited or if he is overheated; however, a high temperature could indicate a medical emergency. On the other hand, if the temperature is below 100 degrees, this could also indicate an emergency.

CAPILLARY REFILL TIME AND GUM COLOR

It is important to know how your dog's gums look when he is healthy, so you will be able to recognize a difference if he is not feeling well. There are a few breeds, among them the Chow Chow and its relatives, that have black gums and a black tongue. This is normal for them. In general, a healthy dog will have bright pink gums. Pale gums are an indication of shock or anemia and are an emergency. Likewise, any yellowish tint is an indication of a sick dog. To check capillary refill time (CRT) press your thumb against the dog's gum. The gum will blanch out (turn white) but should refill (return to the normal pink color) in one to two seconds. CRT is very important.

If the refill time is slow and your dog is acting poorly, you should call your veterinarian immediately.

HEART RATE, PULSE, AND RESPIRATIONS

Heart rate depends on the breed of the dog and his health. Normal heart rates range from about 50 beats per minute in the larger breeds to 130 beats per minute in the smaller breeds. You can take the heart rate by pressing your fingertips on the dog's chest. Count for either 10 or 15 seconds, and then multiply by either 6 or 4 to obtain the rate per minute. A normal pulse is the same as the heart rate and is taken at the femoral artery located on the insides of both rear legs. Respirations should be observed and depending on the size and breed of the dog should be 10 to 30 per minute. Obviously, illness or excitement could account for abnormal rates.

PREPARING FOR AN EMERGENCY

It is a good idea to prepare for an emergency by making a list and keeping it by the phone. This list should include:

1. Your veterinarian's name, address, phone number, and office hours.

Keeping a list by the phone for emergencies can save this little Yorkshire puppy's life.

2. Your veterinarian's policy for after-hour care. Does he take his own emergencies or does he refer them to an emergency clinic?
3. The name, address, phone number and hours of the emergency clinic your veterinarian uses.
4. The number of the National Poison Control Center for Animals in Illinois: 1-800-548-2423. It is open 24 hours a day.

In a true emergency, time is of the essence. Some signs of an emergency may be:

1. Pale gums or an abnormal heart rate.
2. Abnormal temperature, lower than 100 degrees or over 104 degrees.
3. Shock or lethargy.
4. Spinal paralysis.

A dog hit by car needs to be checked out and probably should have radiographs of the chest and abdomen to rule out pneumothorax or ruptured bladder.

EMERGENCY MUZZLE

An injured, frightened dog may not even recognize his owner and may be inclined to bite. If your dog should be injured, you may need to muzzle him to protect yourself before you try to handle him. It is a good idea to practice muzzling the calm, healthy dog so you understand the technique. Slip a lead over his head for control. You can tie his mouth shut with something like a two-foot-long bandage or piece of cloth. A necktie, stocking, leash or even a piece of rope will also work.

1. Make a large loop by tying a loose knot in the middle of the bandage or cloth.
2. Hold the ends up, one in each hand.
3. Slip the loop over the dog's muzzle and lower jaw, just behind his nose.
4. Quickly tighten the loop so he can't open his mouth.
5. Tie the ends under his lower jaw.
6. Make a knot there and pull the ends back on each side of his face, under the ears, to the back of his head.

If he should start to vomit, you will need to remove the muzzle immediately. Otherwise, he could aspirate vomitus into his lungs.

ANTIFREEZE POISONING

Antifreeze in the driveway is a potential killer. Because antifreeze is sweet, dogs will lap it up. The active ingredient in antifreeze is ethylene glycol, which causes irreversible kidney damage. If you witness your pet ingesting antifreeze, you should call your veterinarian immediately. He may recommend that you induce vomiting at once by using hydrogen peroxide, or he may recommend a test to confirm antifreeze ingestion. Treatment is aggressive and must be administered promptly if the dog is to live, but you wouldn't want to subject your dog to unnecessary treatment.

BEE STINGS

A severe reaction to a bee sting (anaphylaxis) can result in difficulty breathing, collapse and even death. A symptom of a bee sting is swelling around the muzzle and face. Bee stings are antihistamine responsive. Over-the-counter antihistamines are available. Ask your veterinarian for recommendations on safe antihistamines to use and the doses to administer. You should monitor the dog's gum color and respirations and watch for a decrease in swelling. If your dog is showing signs of anaphylaxis, your veterinarian may need to give him an injection of corticosteroids. It would be wise to call your veterinarian and confirm treatment.

BLEEDING

Bleeding can occur in many forms, such as a ripped dewclaw, a toenail cut too short, a puncture wound, a severe laceration, etc. If a pressure bandage is needed, it must be released every 15-20 minutes. Be careful of elastic bandages since it is easy to apply them too tightly. Any bandage material should be clean. If no regular bandage is available, a small towel or wash cloth can be used to cover the wound and bind it with a necktie, scarf, or something similar. Styptic powder, or even a soft cake of soap, can be used to stop a bleeding toenail. A ripped dewclaw or toenail may need to be cut back by the veterinarian and possibly treated with antibiotics. Depending on their severity, lacerations and puncture wounds may also need professional treatment. Your first thought should be to clean the wound

with peroxide, soap and water, or some other antiseptic cleanser. Don't use alcohol since it deters the healing of the tissue.

BLOAT

Although not generally considered a first aid situation, bloat can occur in a dog rather suddenly. Truly, it is an emergency! Gastric dilatation-volvulus or gastric torsion—the twisting of the stomach to cut off both entry and exit, causing the organ to "bloat," is a disorder primarily found in the larger, more deep-chested breeds. It is life threatening and requires immediate veterinary assistance.

BURNS

If your dog gets a chemical burn, call your veterinarian immediately. Rinse any other burns with cold water and if the burn is significant, call your veterinarian. It may be necessary to clip the hair around the burn so it will be easier to keep clean. You can cleanse the wound on a daily basis with saline and apply a topical antimicrobial ointment, such as silver sulfadiazine 1 percent cream or gentamicin cream. Burns can be debilitating, especially to an older pet.

They can cause pain and shock. It takes about three weeks for the skin to slough after the burn and there is the possibility of permanent hair loss.

CARDIOPULMONARY RESUSCITATION (CPR)

Check to see if your dog has a heart beat, pulse and spontaneous respiration. If his pupils are already dilated and fixed, the prognosis is less favorable. This is an emergency situation that requires two people to administer lifesaving techniques. One person needs to breathe for the dog while the other person tries to establish heart rhythm. Mouth to mouth resuscitation starts with two initial breaths, one to one and a half seconds in duration. After the initial breaths, breathe for the dog once after every five chest compressions. (You do not want to expand the dog's lungs while his chest is being compressed.) You inhale, cover the dog's nose with your mouth, and exhale *gently*. You should see the dog's chest expand. Sometimes, pulling the tongue forward stimulates respiration. You should be ventilating the dog 12-20 times per minute. The person managing the chest compressions should have the dog lying on his right side with one hand on either side of the dog's chest, directed over the heart between the fourth and fifth ribs (usually this is the point of the flexed elbow). The number of compressions administered depends on the size of the patient. Attempt 80-120 compressions per minute. Check for spontaneous respiration and/or heart beat. If present, monitor the patient and discontinue resuscitation. If you haven't already done so, call your veterinarian at once and make arrangements to take your pet in for professional treatment.

CHOCOLATE TOXICOSIS

Dogs like chocolate, but chocolate kills dogs. Its two basic chemicals, caffeine and theobromine, overstimulate the dog's nervous system. Ten ounces of milk chocolate can kill a 12-pound dog. Symptoms of poisoning include restlessness, vomiting, increased heart rate, seizure, and coma. Death is possible. If your dog has ingested chocolate, you can give syrup of ipecac at a dosage of one-eighth of a teaspoon per pound to induce vomiting. Two tablespoons of hydrogen peroxide is an alternative treatment.

CHOKING

You need to open the dog's mouth to see if any object is visible. Try to hold him upside down to see if the object can be dislodged. While you are working on your dog, call your veterinarian, as time may be critical.

DOG BITES

If your dog is bitten, wash the area and determine the severity of the situation. Some bites may need immediate attention, for instance, if it is bleeding profusely or if a lung is punctured. Other bites may be only superficial scrapes. Most dog bite cases need to be seen by the veterinarian, and some may require antibiotics. It is important that you learn if the offending dog has had a rabies vaccination. This is important for your dog, but also for you, in case you are the victim. Wash the wound and call your doctor for further instructions. You should check on your tetanus vaccination history. Rarely, and I mean rarely, do dogs get tetanus. If the offending dog is a stray, try to confine him for observation. He will need to be confined for ten days. A dog that has bitten a human and is not current on his rabies vacci-

These two Yorkies are having fun in the tub. Never leave your dog unsupervised in the bathtub or any other place where he could drown.

nation cannot receive a rabies vaccination for ten days. Dog bites should be reported to the Board of Health.

DROWNING

Remove any debris from the dog's mouth and swing the dog, holding him upside down. Stimulate respiration by pulling his tongue forward. Administer CPR if necessary, and call your veterinarian. Don't give up working on the dog. Be sure to wrap him in blankets if he is cold or in shock.

ELECTROCUTION

You may want to look into puppy proofing your house by installing GFCIs (Ground Fault Circuit Interrupters) on your electrical outlets. A GFCI just saved my dog's life. He had pulled an extension cord into his crate and was "teething" on it at seven years of age. The GFCI kept him from being electrocuted. Turn off the current before touching the dog. Resuscitate him by administering CPR and pulling his tongue forward to stimulate respiration. Try mouth-to-mouth breathing if the dog is not breathing. Take him to your veterinarian as soon as possible since electrocution can cause internal problems,

such as lung damage, which need medical treatment.

EYES

Red eyes indicate inflammation, and any redness to the upper white part of the eye (sclera) may constitute an emergency. Squinting, cloudiness to the cornea, or loss of vision could indicate severe problems, such as glaucoma, anterior uveitis and episcleritis. Glaucoma is an emergency if you want to save the dog's eye. A prolapsed third eyelid is abnormal and is a symptom of an underlying problem. If something should get in your dog's eye, flush it out with cold water or a saline eye wash. Epiphora and allergic conjunctivitis are annoying and frequently persistent problems. Epiphora (excessive tearing) leaves the area below the eye wet and sometimes stained. The wetness may lead to a bacterial infection. There are numerous causes (allergies, infections, foreign matter, abnormally located eyelashes and adjacent facial hair that rubs against the eyeball, defects or diseases of the tear drainage system, birth defects of the eyelids, etc.) and the treatment is based on the cause. Keeping the hair around the eye cut short and sponging the eye daily will give relief. Many cases are responsive to medical treatment. Allergic conjunctivitis may be a seasonal problem if the dog has inhalant allergies (e.g., ragweed), or it may be a year 'round problem. The conjunctiva becomes red and swollen and is prone to a bacterial infection associated with mucus accumulation or pus in the eye. Again keeping the hair around the eyes short will give relief. Mild corticosteroid drops or ointment will also give relief. The underlying problem should be investigated.

FISH HOOKS

An imbedded fish hook will probably need to be removed by the veterinarian. More than likely, sedation will be required along with antibiotics. Don't try to remove it yourself. The shank of the hook will need to be cut off in order to push the other end through.

FOREIGN OBJECTS

I can't tell you how many chicken bones my first dog ingested. Fortunately she had a "cast iron stomach" and never suffered the consequences. However, she was always going to the veterinarian for treatment. Not all dogs are so lucky. It is unbelievable what some

dogs will take a liking to. I have assisted in surgeries in which all kinds of foreign objects were removed from the stomach and/or intestinal tract. Those objects included socks, pantyhose, stockings, clothing, diapers, sanitary products, plastic, toys, and, last but not least, rawhides. Surgery is costly and not always successful, especially if it is performed too late. If you

This electrical outlet is too close to the dog's crate. A dog could pull the cord into the crate and chew on it, which would electrocute him.

see or suspect your dog has ingested a foreign object, contact your veterinarian immediately. He may tell you to induce vomiting or he may have you bring your dog to the clinic immediately. Don't induce vomiting without the veterinarian's permission, since the object may cause more damage on the way back up than it would if you allow it to pass through.

HEATSTROKE

Heatstroke is an emergency! The classic signs are rapid, shallow breathing; rapid heartbeat; a temperature above 104 degrees; and subsequent collapse. The dog needs to be cooled as quickly as possible and treated immediately by the veterinarian. If possible, spray him down with cool water and pack ice around his head, neck, and groin. Monitor his temperature and stop the cooling process as soon as his temperature reaches 103 degrees. Nevertheless, you will need to keep monitoring his temperature to be sure it doesn't elevate again. If the temperature continues to drop to below 100 degrees, it could be life threatening. Get professional help immediately. Prevention is more successful than treatment. Those at the greatest risk are brachycephalic

(short nosed) breeds, obese dogs, and those that suffer from cardiovascular disease. Dogs are not able to cool off by sweating as people can. Their only way is through panting and radiation of heat from the skin surface. When stressed and exposed to high environmental temperature, high humidity, and poor ventilation, a dog can suffer heatstroke very quickly. Many people do not realize how quickly a car can overheat. Never leave a dog unattended in a car. It is even against the law in some states. Also, a brachycephalic, obese, or infirm dog should never be left unattended outside during inclement weather and should have his activities curtailed. Any dog left outside, by law, must be assured adequate shelter (including shade) and fresh water.

POISONS

Try to locate the source of the poison (the container which lists the ingredients) and call your veterinarian immediately. Be prepared to give the age and weight of your dog, the quantity of poison consumed and the probable time of ingestion. Your veterinarian will want you to read off the ingredients. If you can't reach him, you can call a

To avoid heatstroke, you should provide your Yorkshire Terrier with a shaded area to retreat to when he is outdoors in hot weather.

local poison center or the National Poison Control Center for Animals in Illinois, which is open 24 hours a day. Their phone number is 1-800-548-2423. There is a charge for their service, so you may need to have a credit card number available.

Symptoms of poisoning include muscle trembling and weakness, increased salivation, vomiting and loss of bowel control. There are numerous household toxins (over 500,000). A dog can be poisoned by toxins in the garbage. Other poisons include pesticides, pain relievers, prescription drugs, plants, chocolate, and cleansers. Since I own small dogs I don't have to worry about my dogs jumping up to the kitchen counters, but when I owned a large breed she would clean the counter, eating all the prescription medications.

Your pet can be poisoned by means other than directly ingesting the toxin. Ingesting a rodent that has ingested a rodenticide is one example. It is possible for a dog to have a reaction to the pesticides used by exterminators. If this is suspected you should contact the exterminator about the potential dangers of the pesticides used and their side effects.

Don't give human drugs to your dog unless your veterinarian has given his approval. Some human medications can be deadly to dogs.

POISONOUS PLANTS

Amaryllis (bulb)	Jerusalem
Andromeda	Cherry
Apple Seeds (cyanide)	Jimson Weed
Arrowgrass	Laburnum
Avocado	Larkspur
Azalea	Laurel
Bittersweet	Locoweed
Boxwood	Marigold
Buttercup	Marijuana
Caladium	Mistletoe
Castor Bean	(berries)
Cherry Pits	Monkshood
Chokecherry	Mushrooms
Climbing Lily	Narcissus (bulb)
Crown of Thorns	Nightshade
Daffodil (bulb)	Oleander
Daphne	Peach
Delphinium	Philodendron
Dieffenbachia	Poison Ivy
Dumb Cane	Privet
Elderberry	Rhododendron
Elephant Ear	Rhubarb
English Ivy	Snow on
Foxglove	the Mountain
Hemlock	Stinging Nettle
Holly	Toadstool
Hyacinth (bulb)	Tobacco
Hydrangea	Tulip (bulb)
Iris (bulb)	Walnut
Japanese Yew	Wisteria
Jasmine (berries)	Yew

This list was published in the American Kennel Club *Gazette*, February, 1995. As the list states these are common poisonous plants, but this list may not be complete. If your dog ingests a poisonous plant, try to identify it and call your veterinarian. Some plants cause more harm than others.

PORCUPINE QUILLS
Removal of quills is best left up to your veterinarian since it can be quite painful. Your unhappy dog would probably appreciate being sedated for the removal of the quills.

SEIZURE (CONVULSION OR FIT)
Many breeds, including mixed breeds, are predisposed to seizures, although a seizure may be secondary to an underlying medical condition. Usually a seizure is not considered an emergency unless it lasts longer than ten minutes. Nevertheless, you should notify your veterinarian. Dogs do not swallow their tongues. Do not handle the dog's mouth since your dog probably cannot control his actions and may inadvertently bite you. The seizure can be mild; for instance, a dog can have a seizure standing up. More frequently the dog will lose consciousness and may urinate and/or defecate. The best thing you can do for your dog is to put him in a safe place or to block off the stairs or areas where he can fall.

SEVERE TRAUMA

See that the dog's head and neck are extended so if the dog is unconscious or in shock, he is able to breathe. If there is any vomitus, you should try to get the head extended down with the body elevated to prevent vomitus from being aspi-rated. Alert your veterinarian that you are on your way.

after severe fright. Other causes of shock are hemor-rhage, fluid loss, sepsis, tox-ins, adrenal insufficiency, car-diac failure, and anaphylaxis. The symptoms are a rapid weak pulse, shallow breath-ing, dilated pupils, subnormal temperature, and muscle

It is best to keep your Yorkshire Terrier calm and comfortable when waiting in the veterinarian's office, especially in potentially serious situations.

SHOCK

Shock is a life threatening condition and requires imme-diate veterinary care. It can occur after an injury or even

weakness. The capillary refill time (CRT) is slow, taking longer than two seconds for normal gum color to return. Keep the dog warm while transporting him to the vet-erinary clinic. Time is critical for survival.

A security gate will keep your Yorkshire Terrier safely confined to one area of the house when you are not at home. There are many different types available at your local pet shop.

SKUNKS

Skunk spraying is not necessarily an emergency, although it would be in my house. If the dog's eyes are sprayed, you need to rinse them well with water. One remedy for deskunking the dog is to wash him in tomato juice and follow with a soap and water bath. The newest remedy is bathing the dog in a mixture of one quart of three percent hydrogen peroxide, quarter cup baking soda, and one teaspoon liquid soap. Rinse well. There are also commercial products available.

SNAKE BITES

It is always a good idea to know what poisonous snakes reside in your area. Rattlesnakes, water moccasins, copperheads, and coral snakes are residents of some areas of the United States. Pack ice around the area that is bitten and call your veterinarian immediately to alert him that you are on your way. Try to identify the snake or at least be able to describe it (for the use of antivenin). It is possible that he may send you to another clinic that has the proper antivenin.

TOAD POISONING

Bufo toads are quite deadly. You should find out if these nasty little critters are native to your area.

VACCINATION REACTION

Once in a while, a dog may suffer an anaphylactic reaction to a vaccine. Symptoms include swelling around the muzzle, extending to the eyes. Your veterinarian may ask you to return to his office to determine the severity of the reaction. It is possible that your dog may need to stay at the hospital for a few hours during future vaccinations.

RECOMMENDED READING

DR. ACKERMAN'S DOG BOOKS FROM T.F.H.

OWNER'S GUIDE TO DOG HEALTH
TS-214, 432 pages
Over 300 color photographs

Winner of the 1995 Dog Writers Association of America's Best Health Book, this comprehensive title gives accurate, up-to-date information on all the major disorders and conditions found in dogs. Completely illustrated to help owners visualize signs of illness, different states of infection, procedures and treatment, it covers nutrition, skin disorders, disorders of the major body systems (reproductive, digestive, respiratory), eye problems, vaccines and vaccinations, dental health and more.

SKIN & COAT CARE FOR YOUR DOG
TS-249, 224 pages
Over 200 color photographs

Dr. Ackerman, a specialist in the field of dermatology and a Diplomate of the American College of Veterinary Dermatology, joins 14 of the world's most respected dermatologists and other experts to produce an extremely helpful manual on the dog's skin. Coat and skin problems are extremely common in the dog, and owners need to better understand the conditions that affect their dogs' coats. The book details everything from the basics of parasites and mange to grooming techniques, medications, hair loss and more.

DOG BEHAVIOR AND TRAINING
Veterinary Advice for Owners
TS-252, 292 pages
Over 200 color photographs

Joined by co-editors Gary Landsberg, DVM and Wayne Hunthausen, DVM, Dr. Ackerman and about 20 experts in behavioral studies and training set forth a practical guide to the common problems owners experience with their dogs. Since behavioral disorders are the number-one reason for owners to abandon a dog, it is essential for owners to understand how the dog thinks and how to correct him if he misbehaves. The book covers socialization, selection, rewards and punishment, puppy-problem prevention, excitable and disobedient behaviors, sexual behaviors, aggression, children, stress and more.

RECOMMENDED READING

OTHER DOG BOOKS FROM T.F.H.

THE BOOK OF THE YORKSHIRE TERRIER
by Joan McDonald Brearley

H-1056, 300 pages
Color & b/w photographs
The Book of the Yorkshire Terrier provides
practical advice and much more. In addition to
valuable information about grooming, breeding,
showing, training, and routine maintenance, the
book offers a wealth of fascinating text dealing
with the history of the breed and its developers,
highlighted with hundreds of enchanting
photographs.

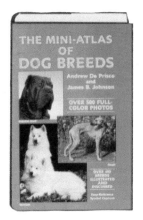

THE MINI-ATLAS OF DOG BREEDS
by Andrew De Prisco and James B. Johnson

H-1106, 544 pages
over 500 full-color photographs
The Mini-Atlas of Dog Breeds written by the
authors of *The Most Complete Dog Book Ever
Published* has been recommended by most national
dog publications for its utility and reader-friendliness.
It is the only accurate field guide for dog lovers.

THE MOST COMPLETE DOG BOOK
EVER PUBLISHED
(A CANINE LEXICON)
by Andrew De Prisco and James B. Johnson

TS-175, 896 pages
Over 1300 full-color photos
This book is an up-to-date encyclopedic
dictionary for the dog person. It is the most
complete single volume on the dog ever published,
covering more dog breeds than any other book as
well as other relevant topics, including health,
showing, training, breeding, anatomy, veterinary
terms, and much more.